MW00988162

THE MINISTRY
OF
PEACE AND JUSTICE

Michael Jordan Laskey

LITURGICAL PRESS
Collegeville, Minnesota

www.litpress.org

Dedicated to the parishes
of the Diocese of Camden

	2	3	4	5	6	7	8	9

Library of Congress Control Number: 2015950491

ISBN: 978-0-8146-4813-1   978-0-8146-4838-4 (ebook)

Contents

1

The Ministry of Peace and Justice

Love in Action

Imagine that the pope has asked you to come up with a one-sentence mission statement for the Catholic Church. What do you write?

You could go in any number of directions, to be sure, but a good place to start might be one of the Gospel of Matthew's most famous scenes (22:35-40), in which a gang of Pharisees tries to corner Jesus. A lawyer in the group asks, "Teacher, which commandment in the law is the greatest?" He thinks that no matter which of the 613 commandments from Hebrew Scripture Jesus picks, the Pharisees will be able to find a different one that is more important, and Jesus will be revealed as a fraud.

Even though he has been put on the spot unfairly, Jesus does not evade the question or waffle. He fires back without hesitation. " 'You shall love the Lord your God with all your heart, and with all your soul, and with all your mind.' This is the greatest and first commandment," he says, quoting from the book of Deuteronomy, before adding another commandment from Leviticus: "And a second is like it: 'You shall love your neighbor as yourself.' On these two commandments hang all the law and the prophets." In the Gospel account, the Pharisees are left speechless.

Jesus proclaims that it's all about love for him, and as followers of Jesus, we're meant to make his priorities our priorities. So, maybe a mission statement for the church like "We strive to love God and our neighbors as ourselves" would work well. Everything we do in our faith communities should flow from—and center on—love of God and neighbor. This is nothing new or revolutionary. But the trick is that Jesus' two love-commandments are as difficult to live out as they are easy to remember!

What Does Jesus Mean by "Love"? Who Does Jesus Mean by "Neighbor"?

Jesus' use of the word "love" itself is the first big challenge. We say "love" all the time: I love my family, I love God, I love college football, I love pizza. In pop culture, love is often reduced to a feeling of affection in one's heart that is subject to change. (See, for example, singer-songwriter Taylor Swift's continuing cycle of love songs followed by breakup songs.)

When Jesus says "love," however, what is he talking about? And who does he mean by "neighbor"? Almost every page of the gospels offers answers to both these questions. Over and over again, Jesus offers a healing touch and listening ear to those who are suffering and pushed to the peripheries of society: lepers, tax collectors, prostitutes, the disabled, criminals, and more. He loves by making outcasts his neighbors and spending time with them.

Jesus is the perfect embodiment of *compassion*, another word that has lost its true meaning. The great theologian Henri Nouwen writes with his coauthors in their book *Compassion* that the word literally means "to suffer with," or to be present to the suffering of others instead of turning away. "Compassion asks us to go where it hurts, to enter into the places of pain, to share in brokenness, fear, confusion, and anguish. Compassion challenges us to cry out with those in misery, to mourn with those who are lonely, to weep with those in tears," they write.[1] For Jesus, to love is to notice the woundedness of others and to say, "I'm not going anywhere. I'm with you."

Not only does Jesus love by spending time with the suffering, but he *is* the suffering. Toward the end of Matthew's gospel (25:31-46), in one of his most pointed stories, Jesus encourages his followers to love by seeing his face in the poor and responding. In the passage, Jesus describes the Last Judgment to his disciples. At the end of time, like a shepherd, he will place all people before him, and separate them into groups of sheep and goats. Jesus places the sheep on his right and the goats on his left, turns to the sheep, and welcomes them into heaven: "For I was hungry and you gave me food, I was thirsty and you gave me something to drink, I was a stranger and you welcomed me, I was naked and you gave me clothing, I was sick and you took care of me, I was in prison and you visited me."

The sheep are grateful and excited, but confused. They don't think they've ever seen Jesus before. How could they have ministered to his needs? Jesus says, "Truly I tell you, just as you did it to one of the least of these who are members of my family, you did it to me." The goats aren't so lucky. Jesus condemns them, for they did not serve him when he was hungry, thirsty, a stranger, naked, ill, or in prison: "Truly I tell you, just as you did not do it to one of the least of these, you did not do it to me." They are sent away to eternal punishment.

There are two radical things about this passage I sometimes forget because the story is so familiar. First, our salvation is directly related to how we respond to the needs of our sisters and brothers. This doesn't mean that we are supposed to do good things and hope God notices, as if he were a cosmic Santa Claus. Instead, it is a powerful reminder that the sort of love Jesus is talking about involves action with and for those who are pushed to society's margins.

Second, when Jesus says, "just as you did it to one of the least of these who are members of my family, you did it to me," he is making a one-to-one identification with those who are hungry, thirsty, far from home. He is *not* saying that we do something good on his *behalf* when we feed the hungry. He is saying we feed Jesus himself. So if you want to see Jesus, look into the face of someone who is suffering. This is "Christ in his most distressing disguise," as Mother Teresa would say.

Christ's sharing in the suffering of others is most powerful on the cross, beautifully described in the hymn in St. Paul's Letter to the Philippians: "[Christ], though he was in the form of God, / did not regard equality with God / as something to be exploited, / but emptied himself . . . he humbled himself / and became obedient to the point of death— / even death on a cross" (2:6-8). In reflecting on this passage, a favorite teacher of mine likes to say that this is not what he would've done if he were the son of God. Instead, he would've worn a sash and rode on a float in the Rose Parade, zapping people he didn't like. Christ could've exercised his omnipotence this way. Instead, he gives up his power, his prestige, and even his life out of love for us. Love, for Jesus, is not primarily a feeling of the heart, but lived out through actions on behalf of others, most particularly those who are suffering and forgotten.

What Is the Ministry of Peace and Justice?

As disciples are meant to make Christ's priorities our priorities, it is our job to work with God to bring his compassion to a wounded world in a wide variety of ways. We'll call this work of outward-reaching love "the ministry of peace and justice."

As this book is called *The Ministry of Peace and Justice*, it's worth including a brief note on what those words mean in a Catholic context.

First, peace. In a Catholic Christian context, peace means a lot more than just "the absence of war or violence." Perhaps a better word for what we really mean by peace is the Hebrew word *shalom*, which not only means an absence of discord, but implies wholeness and togetherness. "The webbing together of God, humans, and all creation in justice, fulfillment, and delight is what the Old Testament prophets called shalom," writes theologian Cornelius Plantinga Jr.[2] "We call it peace, but it means far more than mere peace of mind or cease-fire among enemies.

In the Bible shalom means universal flourishing, wholeness, and delight—a rich state of affairs that inspires joyful wonder as its Creator and Savior opens doors and welcomes the creatures in whom he delights."

Shalom is what is waiting for God's children in heaven, but is also God's dream for us here on Earth. The hope that God's love will overcome human divides and bring peoples together inspires all ministry in this area.

Second, justice. Or, more specifically, social justice. In a CST context, "social justice" is often paired with "charity"—two essential concepts that are on different sides of the same coin. One popular way to illustrate the difference between charity and social justice is the "Babies in the River" story.

Imagine you and some friends are hiking near a river. You pause for a break near a tall waterfall, which rises up above you. As you admire the view, you suddenly notice something disturbing: a baby, floating all by himself, falls over the waterfall. You swim out into the river, pick up the baby, and bring him to safety. One of your friends brings the baby to a hospital, and another joins you in the river. Shockingly, two more babies come over the waterfall, and so you repeat the process. You use your cell phone to call for help, and teams made up of emergency personnel and volunteers take turns watching for babies and rescuing any who come over the waterfall. At a town meeting to discuss the problem, someone stands up and says, "It's great we have so many people helping to pull the babies out of the river. But someone should go upstream to find out what's happening and see if we can stop these babies from falling into the water in the first place!"

In the story, "charity" is represented by those pulling babies out of the river. They are meeting an immediate, dire need. Types of organizations that focus primarily on charity include soup kitchens, food banks, emergency homeless shelters, and home rehab organizations like Habitat for Humanity. As long as people are in need, charitable efforts are required.

"Social justice," on the other hand, is going upstream to address the problem at its root. Justice seeks long-term solutions to social ills that can impact whole communities. Some examples of justice work include advocating to extend legal protection to unborn children, communities working to improve their own education systems, and contacting lawmakers to urge them to protect social programs that help the poor lift themselves out of poverty. The Catholic bishops of the US call charity and justice together "The Two Feet of Love in Action." We need both.

Parish-based peace and justice ministry can help to coordinate charitable efforts, but it also must help parishioners understand what a Catholic conception of social justice is and provide opportunities to act on that knowledge.

Another important definition of social justice is "right relationship." As all humans are brothers and sisters, social justice is about building positive relationships of mutuality and kinship. Even in charitable works, justice is done when the "doer" of the charity does not see him- or herself as better or higher than the "receiver." "Serving others is good. It's a start," writes Gregory Boyle, SJ, in his memoir *Tattoos on the Heart*. "But it's just the hallway that leads to the Grand Ballroom. Kinship—not serving the other, but being one with the other. Jesus was not a 'man for others'; he was one with them. There is a world of difference in that."[3]

Pope Francis Has Renewed the Call to the Ministry of Peace and Justice

The ministry of peace and justice has deep roots in Catholic tradition, but there is new energy around the work, thanks to Pope Francis. Just a month after his election, a pastor in the diocese where I work invited me to talk about peace and justice ministry at his parish. "Well, if Pope Francis is talking so much about it, we should probably do something!" he told me.

From his first days on the job, Francis has emphasized the importance of sharing in Christ's work of compassion on the peripheries of society in the world today. He often talks about the pervasiveness of a modern "throwaway culture," in which not only disposable goods like food are wasted, but people themselves are thrown away because they are seen as unnecessary. Victims of our throwaway culture make up a twenty-first-century list of Jesus' neighbors in the gospel: the unborn child, the working-poor single mother, the immigrant seeking a better life, the girl nearing death from malnutrition.

Our faith-filled response to the throwaway culture, Francis suggests, is to create a "culture of encounter," in which disciples build relationships with those who are often ignored. "[O]nly those able to reach out to others are capable of bearing fruit, creating bonds of communion, radiating joy and being peacemakers," Francis told a gathering of diplomats to the Holy See.[4] In a culture of encounter, big, abstract issues like poverty and immigration reform become names, faces, stories, and relationships. These relationships can change our hearts more than a statistic ever could.

Building a culture of encounter isn't easy. Compassion is uncomfortable because suffering is uncomfortable. It's tempting to turn away from the poor and vulnerable, especially when, in our individualistic culture, we are almost expected to say, "It's not my problem." We have constructed social and economic barriers that keep us separated from those who are different from ourselves. (Think of the "white flight" phenomenon that has left so many of our American cities and suburbs harshly segregated.)

The challenge of building a culture of encounter is the subject of a powerful YouTube video produced by a homeless shelter in New York City. In the video, titled "Have the Homeless Become Invisible?," several different people are interviewed about particular family members who are important to them—a wife, a cousin, a sibling.[5] Little did they know that as they walked through the city streets to the interview, each person passed by that same relative, dressed as a homeless person sitting on the sidewalk. After talking about their family member, each interviewee is shown a video recorded by a hidden camera, capturing the moment they passed their relative without noticing. "Change how you see the homeless," text on the screen reads at the end of the video.

This sort of perspective shift is exactly what Pope Francis is after when he talks about encounter. The key is to see those who are pushed to the edges of society as our own family members—as deeply connected to us as our own biological relatives. The first two words of Christianity's most famous prayer, "Our Father," assert that we all share the same heavenly father, and are therefore brothers and sisters with all people. Because of this belief, Francis wrote in his 2014 World Day of Peace message, "the other is welcomed and loved as a son or daughter of God, as a brother or sister, not as a stranger, much less as a rival or even an enemy." The ministry of peace and justice is about broadening our sense of family.

The Parish Is the Ideal Home for the Ministry of Peace and Justice

There are so many amazing examples of Catholics rising up to the challenge of building kinship across boundaries throughout our history. Many of our saints and other faith heroes made their homes on society's margins, inspired by Christ's example: St. Francis of Assisi, St. Vincent de Paul and St. Louise de Marillac, St. Martin de Porres, St. Frances Cabrini, St. Damien of Molokai, Blessed Archbishop Oscar Romero, Dorothy Day, and Blessed Teresa of Calcutta, just to name a handful. Also, as an institution that shows what it values by creating organizations, the church's network of schools, hospitals, and social service agencies—usually founded to serve the needs of poor communities—is unparalleled.

But these examples of compassion within the Catholic tradition do not mean that our parishes are off the hook because others have acted in our name. In fact, in their 1994 document Communities of Salt and Light: Reflections on the Social Mission of the Parish, the US Conference of Catholic Bishops writes, "[W]e are convinced that the local parish is the most important ecclesial setting for sharing and acting on our Catholic social heritage." In other words, while all of our institutions promoting social good are essential, the parish is the very best place in which to build a culture of encounter.

Why does the parish hold such a privileged place when it comes to the ministry of peace and justice? Because "the parish is where the Church lives," the bishops write. "Parishes are communities of faith, of action, and of hope. They are where the gospel is proclaimed and celebrated, where believers are formed and sent to renew the earth. Parishes are the home of the Christian community; they are the heart of our Church." Anything the church values should have a home in the parish, and the bishops remind us that the ministry of peace and justice is "an essential part of the Church's mission."

So yes, it is a duty for Catholic parishes to be deeply engaged in the ministry of peace and justice. But more than an obligation, it is a *privilege* and an *evangelizing opportunity* for our faith communities.

First, the ministry of peace and justice is a privilege. It's empowering and humbling to think that God would call *us* to cooperate with him in the healing of the world. In Caravaggio's masterpiece *The Calling of Saint Matthew*, Jesus points to Matthew, an unpopular, sinful tax collector, and says, "Follow me." Matthew is depicted with an expression of shock, and points to himself incredulously, as if to say, "Who, me? You couldn't possibly mean me. Do you know who I am?" Jesus' steadfast posture confirms his choice: "Yes, I mean you." Christ points to us, too, no matter our shortcomings or insecurities. As an old saying goes, "God does not call the equipped. He equips the called."

Second, it is an *evangelizing opportunity*. The ministry of peace and justice is hands-on, active, and relevant to the world today. It offers a doorway to the faith for those who might not be active in church. It can deepen the spiritual commitment

Caravaggio, *The Calling of Saint Matthew* (1599–1600). Oil on canvas, 340 x 322 cm. Contarelli Chapel, Church of San Luigi dei Francesi, Rome. Licensed under public domain via Wikimedia Commons.

of disciples of every age. I believe this not only because I have seen it work after time in my work as a lay ecclesial minister, but also because it is my own story. As a high school student with wishy-washy feelings toward faith, I went on week-long service trips with my parish youth group during the summer. During one of those trips to an impoverished city just an hour from my wealthy exurban community, our group met students our own age whose lives were so different from our own because of where they had been born. Some of them hoped to be the first person in their family's history to graduate from high school. This stark disparity did not sit right with me, and a fuse was lit. "This can't be what God wants for the world," I remember thinking. The fire started by that spark is still burning today. It changed my life and led me to my vocation.

What and Who This Book Is For

This book is meant to help Catholic parishes act on the opportunity we have to work with God in the repairing of the world. So, if you're a pastor or pastoral associate, liturgist, director of faith formation, youth minister, administrator, or parishioner with a heart for bringing the love of God to our wounded world, this book is for you.

In the next chapter, I'll introduce seven key themes of Catholic social teaching—the central principles of our tradition that provide the road map for all peace and justice ministry. Then, I'll talk about six areas of parish social ministry that the bishops mention in Communities of Salt and Light, which emerge from Catholic social teaching. After that, since the ministry of peace and justice is for everyone in the parish, not just a few committed individuals, I will suggest ways that parish leaders can integrate peace and justice concerns into parish activities and programs that already exist: liturgy and worship; faith formation for children, youth, and adults; sacramental prep and RCIA; and more. I'll highlight examples from parishes all over the country that are doing peace and justice ministry in creative ways. Finally, I'll discuss practical tips for the work of a peace and justice coordinating committee made up of staff and volunteers within a parish, and include six 60–75-minute learning and discussion sessions that such a committee could use in the early days of its existence or to renew its energy and vision.

2

The Peace and Justice Road Map

Catholic Social Teaching

In order to become a licensed taxi driver in London, a candidate has to pass what has been called the most difficult test in the world. The guidebook given to aspiring cabbies in the city describes the qualifications like this: "To achieve the required standard to be licensed as an "All London" taxi driver you will need a thorough knowledge [of] . . . all the streets; housing estates; parks and open spaces; government offices and departments; financial and commercial centres; diplomatic premises; town halls; registry offices; hospitals; places of worship; sports stadiums and leisure centres; airline offices; stations; hotels; clubs; theatres; cinemas; museums; art galleries; schools; colleges and universities; police stations and headquarters buildings; civil, criminal and coroner's courts; prisons; and places of interest to tourists. In fact, anywhere a taxi passenger might ask to be taken."

That's about twenty-five thousand streets, plus countless buildings and landmarks. One taxi driver told a *New York Times* reporter that the driver "was asked the location of a statue, just a foot tall, depicting two mice sharing a piece of cheese."[1] The process of studying for the exam takes thousands of hours and multiple years of work.

In an era of turn-by-turn GPS navigation systems built into every smartphone, the continued existence of the London taxi driver exam suggests that there's something valuable in having an intimate relationship with a road map and the place it illustrates.

Catholic social teaching (CST) is the church's detailed road map for living our shared life in local, national, and global communities. CST guides any peace and justice ministry a parish might undertake, so some basic familiarity with it is important. (You won't need a London-cabbie level of knowledge to coordinate effective peace and justice ministry, thankfully.)

So what, exactly, is CST? CST is a body of writings by popes, bishops, and other faith leaders that strives to answer big questions like:

- What does each and every child of God need to live a good life?
- How might we build communities that provide the conditions for human flourishing for all?
- What are the different threats to the well-being of individuals and communities, and how might we respond to those threats?
- What rights does every person have? What responsibilities do we each have to make sure those rights are protected?

As the church has sought to map out answers to these questions in every age, our Scriptures have been the first place to start. In the Old Testament, we hear that God created every person in his own image (Gen 1:27). This means that for believers, human beings are not merely animals or clumps of cells. Each unique person is a beautiful work of art fashioned by the Creator, and is therefore deserving of the utmost respect. Anytime a person is threatened by violence or neglect or lack of necessities, believers are called to take action.

In the book of Exodus, God tells Moses that God has heard the cries of the enslaved Israelites, and will take their side against the oppressive Pharaoh (3:1-21). As we try our best to imitate God's love in the world today, we should follow God's lead and also side with those who are most vulnerable.

The prophets of the Old Testament "comforted the afflicted and afflicted the comfortable." When the Israelites forgot to care for the widow, the orphan, and the stranger in their midst, the prophets criticized them and called the Israelites to emulate the compassionate God who led them out of slavery (see Isa 58).

In the New Testament, Jesus emphasizes over and over again that to be his disciple means to love God and to love your neighbor with your whole heart. The love Jesus talks about—the love he perfectly modeled on the cross—goes beyond sentimental feelings. This sort of love is marked by self-giving action that puts the needs of others first. He tells us that we will ultimately be judged by how fully we gave ourselves to others, especially to those we encountered who were hungry, thirsty, strangers, naked, ill, or in prison (Matt 25:31-46). When we see someone who is poor and vulnerable, we see who Mother Teresa called "Christ in his most distressing disguise."

Inspired by the countless scriptural examples of how God wants his people to live, Catholic leaders have read the signs of the times with the eyes of faith and responded. These responses make up the documents of CST.

The oldest text in the collection of writings known as CST is an encyclical letter written in 1891 by Pope Leo XIII, *Rerum Novarum*. Written against the backdrop of the Industrial Revolution, Pope Leo supported the rights of workers and decried the awful conditions many factory laborers faced. This was the first time in modern Catholic history that a pope had commented on a specific social issue in such a formal way.

Since 1891, popes and bishops have followed Pope Leo's lead and applied Gospel values to global events and trends. Pope Saint John XXIII, for instance, responded to the Cold War and the threat of nuclear destruction with the encyclical *Pacem in Terris* (1963), which stresses the importance of peaceful, diplomatic negotiation and presents the Catholic vision of human rights and responsibilities. Pope Saint John Paul II, responding to the widespread existence of abortion, euthanasia, and capital punishment around the world, condemned this "culture of death" and called upon people of goodwill to build a "culture of life" in his letter *Evangelium Vitae* (1995). Pope Benedict XVI and Pope Francis have contributed to CST in more recent years, including Pope Francis's 2015 encyclical on caring for God's creation, *Laudato Sì*.

Surveying the vast body of literature that makes up CST, the Catholic bishops of the United States have identified seven primary themes that are addressed often:

1. Life and Dignity of the Human Person
2. Call to Family, Community, and Participation
3. Rights and Responsibilities
4. Option for the Poor and Vulnerable
5. The Dignity of Work and the Rights of Workers
6. Solidarity
7. Care for God's Creation

Life and Dignity of the Human Person

Just a couple of weeks or so after a baby is conceived, when she is the size of an orange seed, her heartbeat is visible.[2] And just a few weeks after that, blueberry-sized, she has arm and leg buds and kidneys. If she continued to grow at this speed for the entire nine months of pregnancy, she'd be one and a half tons at birth.[3] Since she hears her mother's voice more often and clearly than other voices, she'll be able to distinguish it from others on her first day of postnatal life. And as she can taste flavors from the food her mother eats, she'll remember and prefer those flavors when she's out in the world.[4]

I learned these details about the development of the baby in the womb as I waited with my wife for our first child to be born. These amazing facts and figures added context to the miraculous transformation I witnessed in my wife: from no-life to life; from not-mother to mother. Each time I feel an astonishing kick, I think to myself, "There's a *baby* in there!" I'm reduced to wide-eyed exclamations.

CST's emphasis on the protection of human life and dignity is rooted in this miracle. More than a clump of cells, each person from the moment of conception onward bears the mark of a loving creator. We hear this on the first page of the Bible: "So God created humankind in his image, / in the image of God he created them; / male and female he created them" (Gen 1:27). As a child of God, reflecting the divine countenance in his or her own face, each person has inviolable *dignity*—or, each person is deserving of the utmost respect, no matter what.

This teaching underlies the rest of CST. Because each person is sacred, anything that threatens human dignity must be stopped: from poverty to war to abortion to capital punishment. "At the center of all Catholic social teaching are the transcendence of God and the dignity of the human person," the US Catholic bishops wrote in the pastoral letter The Challenge of Peace.[5] "The human person is the clearest reflection of God's presence in the world; all of the Church's work in pursuit of both justice and peace is designed to protect and promote the dignity of every person. For each person not only reflects God, but is the expression of God's creative work and the meaning of Christ's redemptive ministry."

The threats to human life and dignity around the world today are numerous and diverse. Here are just three of them:

First, the legality of abortion-on-demand in the United States since the Roe v. Wade Supreme Court decision of 1973, violating the unborn child's right to life, has led to over 50 million abortions in the US since then.[6] In an interview with NPR, John Carr, the former social justice director for the US Catholic bishops, reflected on talking to nonreligious college students about this bizarre, sad truth. "I told them I had just gotten a picture of my new granddaughter and I said, I've seen her face, I've seen her fingers, I've seen her toes. She has a name, she has a room," Carr said.[7] "The only thing she doesn't have is the right to be born. It was a sonogram. And they said, I never thought of it that way."

Second, thousands of Christians are killed each year around the world because of their faith. Pope Francis called on the international community to not "look the other way" when encountered with these modern-day martyrs.[8]

Third, in a world with plenty of food to eat, millions of children under the age of five die from malnutrition every year. According to the United Nations, "Poor nutrition causes nearly half (45%) of deaths in children under five—3.1 million children each year."[9]

What might a Catholic parish do to promote human life and dignity?

- Send a contingent to the annual March for Life in Washington, DC, each January, or another similar event closer to your own community.

- Collect baby supplies for an organization that serves mothers facing unexpected pregnancies.

- Connect with an organization like Family Promise (www .familypromise.org) that partners with religious congregations to provide temporary housing for homeless families in church buildings.

Call to Family, Community, and Participation

Back to that rapidly growing baby for just a minute, who can distinguish her mother's voice from others on her first day of postnatal life. Some other things about her from her earliest days in the world: She likes to look at faces, prefers happy ones to fearful ones, enjoys eye contact, and prefers her mother's to any other. She can recognize her native language. She can mimic your own facial expressions. She can tell the difference between the cries of newborns and other babies, and is likely to express distress only if another newborn's cry is detected.[10]

Another way to think about it: A baby knows her mother's voice and face before the baby knows she is her own separate person. From their very first days in the world, human beings are social creatures. We were not designed to be alone, but to live in relationship with others, beginning with our family. The CST principle "Call to Family, Community, and Participation" is all about this human truth. CST starts with the sanctity of the individual person, but no person lives in a vacuum. Solutions to social ills are enacted in communities.

Let's take a quick look at each of the three parts of this theme separately.

First, the *call to family*. Families are the basic building blocks for society. "As the family goes, so goes the nation, and so goes the whole world in which we live," said Pope John Paul II.[11] As the fundamental human communities, families are the places where faith and justice are learned and nurtured. CST calls for public policies that support family life, from fair hours for employees so they can spend time with their families to immigration reforms that allow families that have been torn apart by deportation to reunite.

Second, the *call to community*. At the heart of this part of the theme is the concept of the "common good." Commitment to the common good means Catholics are called to resist the temptation to ask, What is the best for me and mine? Instead, we are called to ask, What is the best for all of us? "The obligation to 'love our neighbor' has an individual dimension, but it also requires a broader social commitment to the common good," the US Catholic bishops wrote in the document Economic Justice for All.[12] Considering the common good within an economic context, they continue, "We have many partial ways to measure and debate the health of our economy: Gross National Product, per capita income, stock market prices, and so forth. The Christian vision of economic life looks beyond them all and asks, Does economic life enhance or threaten our life together as a community?"

That question at the end of the quote is a great way to reflect on the common good. You can substitute out the words "economic life" in the sentence and replace them with plenty of others: politics, culture, education system, health care system, housing system, and so on.

Finally, the *call to participation*. The Catholic Church teaches that all people have the right to participate in public life, and that those who have access to that right are called to participate. As politics are the way big decisions are made that impact individuals and communities, CST calls us to be involved. This does not mean that the church gets involved in partisan politics, but that part of our job as Catholics pursuing justice is to lobby our elected officials on behalf of the poor and vulnerable. "If politicians go wherever the wind blows," a Catholic social justice advocate I know likes to say, "then it's our job to change the wind." Catholics answering the "call to participation" stay on top of current events, contact their legislators often to advocate for public policy that lifts up the poor and vulnerable, and vote in elections with a conscience formed by CST.

"In the Catholic Tradition, responsible citizenship is a virtue, and participation in political life is a moral obligation," the US Catholic bishops wrote in the document Forming Consciences for Faithful Citizenship.[13] "This obligation is rooted in our baptismal commitment to follow Jesus Christ and to bear Christian witness in all we do. As the *Catechism of the Catholic Church* reminds us, 'It is necessary that all participate, each according to his position and role, in promoting the common good. This obligation is inherent in the dignity of the human person. . . . As far as possible citizens should take an active part in public life' (nos. 1913–1915)."

Some real-world examples of the call to family, community, and participation include:

Family: As mentioned above, the immigration system in the United States leads to the deportation of parents whose children are US citizens, tearing families apart. Learn more about the church's efforts at advocating for comprehensive immigration reform in the US at www.justiceforimmigrants.org.

Community: The Catholic Campaign for Human Development is a national program that funds dozens of community organizing groups that come together to address pressing social issues in their own cities and towns.

Participation: Nations from El Salvador to Egypt to South Sudan have struggled in recent years to have free and fair elections. The church supports any effort that would allow those living under autocratic regimes to become what Pope Paul VI called "artisans of their own destiny."[14]

What might a parish do to promote the call to family, community, and participation?

- Create community service opportunities for families to participate in together.

- Invite various community agencies in your city or town to participate in a "community fair" at your parish, letting parishioners know about their work and opportunities for connection.

- Leading up to an election, invite small faith-sharing groups to read and discuss the US Catholic bishops' document Forming Consciences for Faithful Citizenship. The document and educational resources are available online at www.faithfulcitizenship.org.

Rights and Responsibilities

Monsignor Oscar Romero was appointed archbishop of San Salvador, El Salvador in 1977 during a time of great civil unrest. An unjust political and economic machine with strong military backing oppressed the poor, who were beginning to rise up to demand fairer treatment.

Romero was known as a quiet, noncontroversial priest, which is why he was appointed to the post. However, something fundamental changed in him when one of his best friends, a Jesuit priest named Rutilio Grande, was assassinated just a few weeks into Archbishop Romero's tenure.

The weekend after Fr. Grande's death, Archbishop Romero cancelled Mass throughout the country and held a single Mass in the city's cathedral. He blamed the government for Fr. Grande's death and demanded justice.[15] Romero's conversion was just beginning.

As other priests and lay Christians were kidnapped and killed, he spoke out with urgency. Night after night, he recorded reflections on the Gospel's call to promote justice for the poor, which were broadcast throughout the country. "The great need today is for Christians who are active and critical, who don't accept situations without analyzing them inwardly and deeply," he said. "We no longer want masses of people like those who have been trifled with for so long. We want persons like fruitful fig trees, who say 'yes' to justice and 'no' to injustice and can make use of the precious gift of life, despite the circumstances."[16]

On March 24, 1980, while celebrating Mass, Archbishop Romero was shot and killed. Just days before, he had said to a magazine, "If they kill me, I will rise again in the people of El Salvador."[17] Through a bloody civil war and continuing oppression, Salvadorans have followed the example of Romero and have spoken out for justice. On May 23, 2015, Oscar Romero was beatified by the Catholic Church, the final step before sainthood.

Archbishop Romero's story illustrates the CST theme "Rights and Responsibilities." First, rights: the Catholic Church teaches that each person has human rights as a child and friend of God. Pope John XXIII outlined these rights in his 1963 encyclical letter *Pacem in Terris*, and they include the right to life, food, clothing, shelter, medical care, work, rest, and necessary social services (11). Further, these rights include access to education, the right to worship freely, and the right to participate in public life.

But along with these rights come responsibilities to make sure those rights are upheld for all. If a person notices another's right to a dignified life is threated somehow, he or she is obligated to act.

Archbishop Romero noticed that the rights of priests and the rights of the poor in El Salvador were being trampled. The death of his friend Fr. Grande snapped his responsibility into focus. As the leader of the church for the country, he decided he had to use his position of authority to speak out on behalf of the poor.

How might a Catholic parish promote human rights and responsibilities as Romero did?

- *Right to life:* Advocate for laws that extend legal protection to unborn children.

- *Right to food:* Support a local organization that works on food security issues with a periodic food drive.

- *Right to participate in public life:* Hold an educational forum to highlight pressing social issues that might be at play in a particular election. (Note: these gatherings must not be partisan or endorse any particular candidate. See the US bishops' document Forming Consciences for Faithful Citizenship for direction.)

Option for the Poor and Vulnerable

As a young, radical journalist in New York City in the 1910s and 1920s, Dorothy Day witnessed the disparity between the lives of wealthy and poor people. She reported on worker strikes and high unemployment in the city. An atheist, Dorothy found herself slowly drawn toward belief when she experienced the beauty and joy of the birth of her daughter, Tamar. The Catholic Church—the church of the masses—appealed to the communal streak in her, and she converted to the faith.

After reporting on a hunger march in Washington, DC, for a Catholic magazine, Dorothy went to the city's National Shrine of the Immaculate Conception. "There I offered up a special prayer, a prayer which came with tears and with anguish, that some way would open up for me to use what talents I possessed for my fellow workers, for the poor," she wrote in her autobiography.[18] Her prayer was answered in a way Dorothy never could have imagined.

Back in New York, she connected with an itinerant Catholic intellectual named Peter Maurin, and together they founded what became known as the Catholic Worker Movement. They established a newspaper that detailed the plight of the working class, and as the poor flocked to them for support, they established a "house of hospitality" to shelter and feed those who were marginalized. Dorothy, Peter, and many who joined the movement gave their lives away to those who were suffering.

"What we would like to do is change the world—make it a little simpler for people to feed, clothe, and shelter themselves as God intended them to do," Dorothy wrote in a 1946 issue of the *Catholic Worker* newspaper.[19] "And, by fighting for better conditions, by crying out unceasingly for the rights of the workers, the poor, of the destitute—the rights of the worthy and the unworthy poor, in other words—we can, to a certain extent, change the world; we can work for the oasis, the little cell of joy and peace in a harried world. We can throw our pebble in the pond and be confident that its ever widening circle will reach around the world."

Their pebble's circle has indeed reached around the world: today, the Catholic Worker Movement is made up of 236 communities "committed to nonviolence, voluntary poverty, prayer, and hospitality for the homeless, exiled, hungry, and forsaken."[20] And the cause for Dorothy Day's sainthood in the Catholic Church was endorsed by the US Catholic bishops in 2012![21]

The life and work of Dorothy Day embody the CST principle "option for the poor and vulnerable" perfectly. A phrase first used by Jesuit priest Pedro Arrupe in 1968,[22] and then adopted by Latin American bishops in the 1970s, the "option for the poor" means that Catholic Christians have an obligation to care for the poor and vulnerable and to work to build societies where the poor are treated justly. The option for the poor means that when we're judging how a particular society is faring, we don't start by looking at how wealthy the well-off are. Instead, we evaluate the society based on how the poor are treated; we look at the well-being of the hungry, the thirsty, the homeless, the stranger, the ill, the imprisoned (see Matt 25:31-46).

The word "option" in this theme of CST doesn't mean "optional"! It does mean, however, that it's up to each of us to choose to work for justice for and with the poor over and over again—just as Dorothy Day and her companions did.

And of course, Dorothy spent her life imitating Christ. "Our faith in Christ, who became poor, and was always close to the poor and the outcast, is the basis of our concern for the integral development of society's most neglected members," Pope Francis wrote in The Joy of the Gospel.[23]

When Catholic leaders speak out about pressing social issues today, almost all of them are somehow connected to the option for the poor and vulnerable:

Valuable domestic social programs that help lift the poor out of poverty, such as the Supplemental Nutrition Assistance Program (food stamps), are constantly on the budgetary chopping block. The US Catholic bishops have called on lawmakers to create a "circle of protection" around these programs.[24]

When they talk about the importance of protecting creation, the US Catholic bishops always describe how environmental degradation has a disproportionately disastrous effect on the poor.[25]

The church calls on all the privileged to "renounce some of their rights so as to place their goods more generously at the service of others."[26] In other words, those with access to more than enough resources to live are called on to live simply so that others may simply live.

What might a Catholic parish do to promote the option for the poor and vulnerable?

- Participate in the annual Catholic Relief Services (CRS) Rice Bowl program during Lent, which funds the US Catholic Church's international development and disaster relief work.

- Send small groups of parishioners to volunteer at a local soup kitchen, homeless shelter, or other community agency that serves and empowers those who are poor and vulnerable.

- Organize a postcard campaign to legislators urging them to create a "circle of protection" around the social programs that help people lift themselves out of poverty.

The Dignity of Work and the Rights of Workers

Tim Harris, who has Down syndrome, owns a restaurant called "Tim's Place" in Albuquerque, New Mexico, which opened in 2010. In addition to serving up breakfast and lunch seven days a week, folks come from all over for a "guilt free, calorie free" item: a hug from Tim himself, which the restaurant tallies on a digital Hug Counter. "I love giving all the customers a hug because I want them to feel comfortable and connected and being around friends," Tim says.

Tim's parents, Keith and Jeanne, encouraged Tim to pursue his dream, and they've become inspirations to families with children with disabilities around the country. "We've had several families with young children with disabilities who have come in or written and said, 'I never thought this would be possible for my son or daughter,'" Jeanne says. "It's changing the way they're thinking as they're raising their young children.[27]

It's no accident that Tim's pursuit of a full, flourishing life includes work. "Work is more than a way to make a living," the US Conference of Catholic Bishops write.[28] "It is a form of continuing participation in God's creation." Since each person is made in the image and likeness of God, the prime Creator, it makes sense that humans would share in that creative instinct.

CST promotes the dignity of work and rights of workers, therefore, because work is a sacred act. CST's special emphasis on work goes all the way back to the first modern CST document, Pope Leo XIII's *Rerum Novarum* (1891), which was written against the backdrop of the Industrial Revolution. As workers were being mistreated, facing dangerous conditions in factories, and being paid an unjust wage, Pope Leo called for fair wages and asserted workers' right to unionize (*Rerum Novarum* 20, 49).

In our time today, various issues concerning the dignity of work and rights of workers continue, including persistent unemployment and underemployment dating back to the economic downturn of 2008; unsafe working conditions and unfair wages for individuals overseas who produce goods that are often consumed here in the West, from clothing to electronic devices; minimum-wage jobs that do not pay a "living wage," forcing many people to work multiple jobs in an attempt to make ends meet; growing economic inequality indicating a decrease in social mobility—many low-income individuals and families are unable to lift themselves out of poverty no matter how hard they work.

What might a Catholic parish do to promote the dignity of work and rights of workers?

- Tap into parishioners' expertise and connections by hosting a professional networking event, resume workshop, or job fair in your community.

- Serve Fair Trade coffee at parish events, which is coffee grown by farmers who are paid a just wage and work in safe conditions. Learn more about Fair Trade at www .crsfairtrade.org.

- Gather a small group of parishioners to visit an area non-profit that helps provide job skills training. Catholic Charities agencies often are engaged in this work.

Solidarity

Along the imposing border fence that divides New Mexico and Texas from Mexico, large crowds have gathered each November since 1999 for a special outdoor Mass. Celebrated by the bishops of three neighboring dioceses—two in the United States and one in Mexico—the Mass started as a ritual of remembrance of the thousands of individuals who have died in their attempt to travel to the United States. "We pray for them as well as those immigrants who are here now but who live in fear of exploitation and deportation daily," Bishop Mark J. Seitz of El Paso told the Catholic News Service in 2014.

The Mass is a true "cross-border experience." An altar is placed next to the fence on each side, symbolizing the belief that unity in Christ overcomes the barriers we build to separate ourselves from others. The first reading is proclaimed on one side of the fence, the second reading on the other. Because the border at the spot where they hold the Mass is marked by a chain-link fence, every part of the Mass is visible from both countries.

At the 2014 Mass, a twelve-year-old girl named Yoryet on the American side locked fingers through the fence with her mother, who had been deported to Mexico after a routine traffic stop seven years earlier. "It's been so long, I need to see her," Yoryet said. "Other children get to see their moms on special occasions like Mother's Day. I don't. It's not fair," she said through tears.[29]

This annual celebration is a wonderful example of the CST principle *solidarity*, which means that because each person is a creation of God, we are all part of one, indivisible human family. The word shares its root with words like "solo" and "solitary": one. We are one.

The barriers we construct to divide our one human family into disconnected groups—by nationality, race, income, and more—are artificial and not of God. Pope John Paul II talked and wrote about solidarity often. "[Solidarity] is not a feeling of vague compassion or shallow distress at the misfortunes of so many people, both near and far," he wrote in the encyclical letter *Sollicitudo Rei Socialis*.[30] "On the contrary, it is a firm and persevering determination to commit oneself to the common good; that is to say, to the good of all and of each individual, because we are all really responsible for all."

We are all really responsible for all. In our Western culture where individualism is lifted up as the ultimate good, solidarity asserts that we are called to care for the well-being of our brothers and sisters around the world. Saint Paul captured our unity as a human family best in his First Letter to the Corinthians: "If one member suffers, all suffer together with it; if one member is honored, all rejoice together with it" (12:26).

The concept of solidarity across man-made borders applies to some crucial social issues:

The Catholic bishops of the United States have repeatedly called on lawmakers to increase poverty-focused international assistance. In a 2015 letter, for instance, representatives of the US bishops and Catholic Relief Services asked Congress to continue funding migration and refugee assistance, support for infectious disease control, and investments in education and agriculture in Central America and the Middle East.[31]

The church emphasizes the importance of peaceful, diplomatic solutions to international conflicts, from the Holy Land to Syria to Sudan.

The Catholic Church has also always been a leading voice for comprehensive immigration reform of the American immigration system, as individuals must have the right to migrate to provide for their families.

Catholic Relief Services is a big supporter of Fair Trade, a movement that helps provide consumers with goods like coffee, chocolate, and jewelry that were grown and produced by fairly paid adults overseas.

What might a Catholic parish do to promote solidarity?

- Partner with Catholic Relief Services to host a Fair Trade sale (www.crsfairtrade.org).

- Establish a "parish twin" relationship with a parish overseas or in your own diocese that emphasizes building relationships across boundaries.

- Encourage parishioners to email legislators about pressing international poverty issues through the "Catholics Confront Global Poverty" network (www.confront globalpoverty.org).

- Host potluck dinner with foods from around the world, and encourage parishioners to bring dishes from their own countries of origin. If a local Catholic Charities agency works to resettle refugees in your area, consider inviting some of these new local residents to attend and bring a dish to share.

Care for God's Creation

Imagine that you are in one of your favorite outdoor places on Earth—a place you know well, and one that comes to mind quickly. Where are you? What is the weather like? What time of day is it? What do you see, hear, feel, and smell? Close your eyes and hold this place in your mind for a moment.

What words would you use to describe the place? What words would you use to describe yourself when you're in that place? Why is it one of your favorites? What about it in particular appeals to you? What memories do you have that are connected to this place?

Spending time in God's creation is a privileged way to learn about God himself. A youth minister I know used to work at a parish that stood in a large field next to a farm, with gently rolling hills on the horizon. "If I got to see the sun set behind those hills just once every ten years, that would be enough to make me believe in God," he told me once. "But I get to see it *every day.*"

Honoring the sacredness of nature has deep roots in Catholic tradition. Saint Francis of Assisi, the patron saint of the environment, offers a great example of this tradition in his magnificent hymn "The Canticle of the Sun": "Be praised, my Lord, through all Your creatures, / especially through my lord Brother Sun, / who brings the day; and You give light through him. / And he is beautiful and radiant in all his splendor! / Of You, Most High, he bears the likeness." In the following stanzas, St. Francis names other elements of creation that reveal God's glory: Sister Moon and the stars, Brothers Wind and Air, Sister Water, Mother Earth. Francis composed the canticle toward the end of his life in the early thirteenth century—about 750 years before the first Earth Day was celebrated! Our faith-based call to care for creation is not some recent development or "go green" trend. Earth is a gift from God, and it's our duty to take care of that gift.

The church's social teaching on the dignity of every person is also connected to how we care for creation. In his encyclical on the environment, *Laudato Sì*, Pope Francis spent a lot of time discussing "human ecology," or the interaction between the natural world and human communities. The Catholic Church cares about global climate change, for instance, because the environmental degradation is already having a big impact on human beings—especially the poor, who struggle to afford food as crop yields shrink and prices skyrocket.[32]

"At its core, global climate change is not about economic theory or political platforms, nor about partisan advantage or interest group pressures. It is about the future of God's creation and the one human family," the US Catholic bishops wrote in 2001.[33] "It is about protecting both 'the human environment' and the natural environment. It is about our human steward-ship of God's creation and our responsibility to those who come after us."

Man-made climate change has already had a negative impact in many ways, including increased occurrence of drought, which affects farmers' ability to grow food to consume and/or sell, and also drives the prices of food up worldwide; and increased inten-sity of extreme weather, such as hurricanes and heat waves, which disproportionately affect those who live in substandard shelter.

What might a Catholic parish do to promote care of God's creation?

- Take the "St. Francis Pledge" to pray, act, and advocate to solve climate change as a parish, or encourage individ-uals to do so on their own. Check out the pledge at www .catholicclimatecovenant.org.

- Organize a study group around Pope Francis's *Laudato Sì* encyclical.

- Discuss and enact ways the parish could have a positive impact on the environment, from reducing energy con-sumption to planting a community garden.

3

Using the Road Map
to Get Somewhere

Six Areas of Peace and Justice Ministry

At the beginning of the last chapter, I described Catholic social teaching (CST) as the church's road map for how we might live our shared life in local, national, and global communities.

As a kid, I remember our family having road maps. Before a vacation, my dad and I might stop by the local AAA agency to pick up a map for the upcoming trip. During the days leading up to the trip, he would unfold the map on the kitchen counter and plot our route. On the road, Mom would be tasked with navigating, which led to occasional moments of what one might charitably call short-term spousal opinion divergence.

A few years later, when I had my own driver's license and needed to go somewhere new, I'd log on to MapQuest, pull up turn-by-turn directions, and print them out. If I didn't have someone riding along with me, I'd try to memorize the turns ahead of time. At the end of my college career, as I prepared to move to a new state, I went to a Circuit City and invested in a GPS unit. I remember giggling with glee at this little box that knew where I was, would tell me where to turn, and recalculate directions if I made a mistake. Now, just seven years after I

purchased it, the GPS languishes unused in my glove compart-
ment. Instead, I use a smartphone app to navigate, which can
anticipate upcoming traffic and change my route on the fly.

If you took away my phone and handed me a road map, it'd
take me a lot of work to adjust. I can only imagine what would
happen if you did the same to a younger driver who has never
driven without GPS.

So if the last chapter was about laying out the CST road map
for inspection, the rest of the book is about using that map to get
somewhere. In other words, if CST is the map, peace and justice
ministry is the driving. This chapter will outline six different specific
areas of peace and justice ministry, which are outlined in the US
Catholic bishops' 1994 document Communities of Salt and Light.[1]

1. Anchoring Social Ministry: Prayer and Worship

2. Sharing the Message: Preaching and Education

3. Serving the "Least of These": Outreach and Charity

4. Advocating for Justice: Legislative Action

5. Creating Community: Organizing for Justice

6. Building Solidarity: Beyond Parish Boundaries

In each section, I'll briefly describe the area of social ministry
and include some practical ways a parish might live it out.

1. Anchoring Social Ministry:[2] Prayer and Worship

"The most important setting for the Church's social teaching
is not in a food pantry or in a legislative committee room, but in
prayer and worship, especially gathered around the altar for the
Eucharist," the bishops write in Communities of Salt and Light.[3]

As the source and summit of our faith, the eucharistic celebration equips us with the spiritual strength necessary to bring
God's love to the world, especially to those who are most hurting. A shared meal to which all are welcome, the Eucharist is also
a stark reminder that there are too many around the world who
go hungry. Pope Benedict XVI made the connection between

Eucharist and peace and justice ministry in his encyclical letter *Deus Caritas Est*: "A Eucharist which does not pass over into the concrete practice of love is intrinsically fragmented," he wrote.[4] The US Catholic bishops have produced a fabulous resource called "Sacraments and Social Mission" that is available for free online and helps to draw even more connections between our sacramental life and peace and justice ministry.[5]

Integrating prayer and worship and peace and justice ministry will help your parish illustrate for parishioners how the social justice work we do springs from our faith and is not an optional element of discipleship. As the bishops write in Communities of Salt and Light, "We see the parish dimensions of social ministry not as an added burden, but as a part of what keeps a parish alive and makes it truly Catholic."

Top 9 Ways to Anchor Peace and Justice Ministry in Prayer and Worship

1. Make sure social justice concerns are included in the general intercessions at Sunday Mass. Rotate through different themes of CST and include an intercession or two each week during the prayers of the faithful. It's best if these intercessions can be connected to current events or special yearly observations. For instance, near the anniversary of the Roe v. Wade Supreme Court decision legalizing abortion, a special intercession for unborn children and their families everywhere would be appropriate.

2. Publish a family-friendly prayer before meals in the parish bulletin and on the parish website. Invite parish families to make sure they include those who are hungry in their pre-meal grace. A sample you could use:

> Merciful God, Giver of Life, you are with us when we are hungry, lonely, or afraid.
> At this table, we taste your new creation, where all people share in your peace.
> Help us to share the gifts of the earth, and help everyone to create a better world,
> Through Christ our Lord, Amen.[6]

3. Make frequent use of your hymnal's selections that have social justice themes. There is a nice collection of "mission and ministry" songs and hymns in every Catholic hymnal that are especially appropriate when a particular Sunday's readings have strong peace and justice connections.

4. Collecting food on a Sunday at church? Have a basket of the food brought up during the offertory. This simple ritual can link the shared meal of the Eucharist to the parish's anti-hunger efforts.

5. Pay attention to the liturgical year and highlight certain saints' connection to peace and justice ministry. Near the feast of St. Francis of Assisi (October 4), for instance, host a blessing of the animals prayer service and invite parishioners to bring their pets. During the prayer service, highlight St. Francis's deep care for the environment and our call to share in that mission. Just a few other key faith figures' feast days you could highlight include:

> Blessed Oscar Romero (March 24)
> St. Damien of Molokai, minister to lepers (May 10)
> Blessed Teresa of Calcutta (September 5)
> St. Vincent de Paul, patron of charities (September 27)
> St. Maximilian Kolbe, patron of prisoners and the pro-life movement (August 14)
> St. Martin de Porres, patron of social justice (November 3)
> St. Frances Xavier Cabrini, patron of immigrants (November 13)

6. Pray on or off the parish campus in connection to urgent social concerns. The annual "Life Chain" day of prayer in October encourages people of faith to publicly pray for unborn children and their families. Immigration reform advocates in Newark, New Jersey, have prayed outside the immigrant detention center there on several Ash Wednesdays. My high school youth ministry program attended a prayer vigil outside of a retail store to pray for exploited workers around the world.

7. Pray before, during, and after any social justice ministry experience. Is a group from the parish going to a food pantry? Gather before the trip to pray for those who are hungry. Pray afterward in thanksgiving for those you met and for the grace to continue bringing God's love to those who suffer. Is a group from the parish going on a weeklong service immersion trip somewhere? Commission and pray for them at a Sunday liturgy right before their departure.

8. Work to make sure your worshiping community walks the talk. Too many times, I've heard stories about families with children with special needs, for example, who feel utterly unwelcome at Mass. If we're going to talk about the need for justice in society, we have to practice justice in our parishes. Do all families feel welcome in the community? Do single parents? Do racial and ethnic minorities? If not, then there's work to be done.

9. Connect peace and justice to sacramental preparation. Could individuals preparing to enter the church through the RCIA participate in a justice or charity initiative together? Are confirmation candidates involved in peace and justice activities in the lead-up to their reception to the sacrament? Are engaged couples, who are getting ready to celebrate a sacrament of service, participating in justice activities as a central element of their preparation? As sacramental preparation is about helping individuals prepare for a life of holistic discipleship, peace and justice activities should be a part of the mix.

2. Sharing the Message: Preaching and Education

"Our social doctrine is an integral part of our faith; we need to pass it on clearly, creatively, and consistently," the bishops write in Communities of Salt and Light. CST "must also be an essential part of the curriculum and life of our schools, religious education programs, sacramental preparation, and Christian initiation activities."

Catholics can't act on CST if they don't know CST. A comprehensive peace and justice ministry at a parish weaves CST into any and all faith formation activities that are taking place: into children's ministry to youth ministry to adult faith formation; into small faith-sharing communities and prayer groups and Scripture studies; into liturgical ministries and even financial ministries.

This means parish staff members and volunteers who are tasked with coordinating various ministries all should have a proficient knowledge of CST and an ability to communicate it creatively in their respective ministry settings. (Chap. 4 covers some strategies for integration.)

Parish Spotlight: Education in Catholic Social Teaching

Parish name: Catholic Community of the Holy Spirit

Location: Mullica Hill and Woodstown, New Jersey

Director of Religious Education:
          Renee Lavender

Activity: Intergenerational "Faith Festival" titled *Faith that is Witnessed: Catholic Social Teaching*

In an email exchange, Renee told me about one of her parish's "faith festivals," which are intergenerational programs that include age-specific breakouts and whole-family activities.

Q: What are some different hands-on activities you included in the "Faith that is Witnessed" faith festival to introduce Catholic social teaching to different age groups?

A: We try and incorporate a different hands-on activity for each grade level once we break into groups or provide at least a different activity for Primary, Middle, and Junior High groups and finally an Intergenerational activity:

The *primary levels* listened to a story concerning our elderly neighbors and ways that help them reconnect with memories. The children colored placemats on which space was made available for individuals to write a memory which made them feel "warm" inside especially during this past winter. These placemats were later delivered to a local retirement village.

The *middle level* listened to a story that highlighted the work of volunteers at a soup kitchen. They then focused on the Corporal Works of Mercy along with designing posters entitled "The ABCs of Stewardship Soup." Students were invited beforehand to bring in cans of soup. These cans were collected and boxed by students and later sent to a food pantry.

Our *junior high level* read an article: "From Manger to Mission—Through Baptism, We Are Sent; Through Eucharist We Are Nourished" by Jeanne Heiberg. They made mobiles that symbolize and recall the mission of Jesus as well as their own mission as disciples of Jesus. They were initially told that something special would be done with the mobiles, and therefore to take extra effort in making. At the end of the session they exchanged with the person across from them. The message was that our mission as disciples is to share our talents and gifts with others.

The *intergenerational* activity included our parish family (preschoolers–grandparents) decorating and filling "Valentine Bags" for the clients of a local food pantry. In the weeks after the faith festival, when individuals came to pick up food from the distribution center, they also received a Valentine Bag for each member of their family. We wanted to impress upon our families that Valentine's Day, a day devoted to love, is more about action than a feeling.

Q: Why do you think young people responded well to these activities?
A: All the groups mentioned they liked the opportunity to work not only in their own leveled groups but also to have the opportunity to share time with other members of our parish community. They appreciated the fact that they were actively involved throughout the evening while working in groups rather than just sitting and listening.

The younger children loved the idea that their contribution was being sent to the retirement village, and the middle-level students enjoyed the fact that their posters were on display and that they were actively involved with the boxing of their soup contribution.

The intergenerational piece seemed to be the most powerful experience for people. Everyone had the opportunity meet and share time together. Even the youngest of children were empowered to decorate, fill, and box the Valentine Bags for the food pantry.

At the end of the evening, all the participants were involved in cleanup of the facility and/or loading the van with boxes of Valentine Bags and soup. It truly was a community building and faith sharing event.

3. Serving the "Least of These": Outreach and Charity

"Parishes are called to reach out to the hurting, the poor, and the vulnerable in our midst in concrete acts of charity," the bishops write. "This is an area of creativity and initiative with a wide array of programs, partnerships with Catholic Charities, and common effort with other churches. Thousands of food pantries; hundreds of shelters; and uncounted outreach programs for poor families, refugees, the elderly, and others in need are an integral part of parish life." (This area of social ministry is concerned with meeting immediate needs of individuals, as described in last chapter's "A Quick Note on 'Peace and Justice.'")

While many parishes I work with are engaged in outreach and charity through food and clothing drives and by providing monetary assistance to individuals or organizations, one step I invite them to take is to get off the parish property to build relationships with those living on society's margins. For instance, one parish transitioned from dropping off casseroles at a local homeless shelter to sending small groups once a month to the shelter to serve and spend time with the clients there.

The Society of St. Vincent de Paul, which connects with those in need through one-on-one in-person visits and provides essential assistance, is one of the Catholic Church's finest examples of charitable ministry.

Parish Spotlight: Outreach and Charity

Parish name: St. Mary Catholic Faith Community

Location: Hales Corners, Wisconsin

Social Concerns Coordinator:
                Pam Lownik

Activity: Go Make a Difference outreach initiative
                (GoMAD)

Founded in response to the homelessness problem in nearby Milwaukee, St. Mary's GoMAD initiative connects the parish with six different agencies that are doing the "heavy lifting" in the community, including a daytime shelter, a homeless veterans program, and a youth-oriented homelessness center. All parishioners are encouraged to get involved somehow with at least one of the agencies.

While financial contributions and canned-goods donations to support the organizations are part of the initiative, the real success of GoMAD is the relationships it fosters. Many parishioners take part in ongoing, onsite service projects and legislative advocacy on their homeless friends' behalf. Parish teens connect with homeless youth through the initiative and build relationships with them through shared prayer, conversation, and activities. One adult parishioner has taught sewing to homeless women every week for a few years. Parish school eighth graders worked with a shelter to start a community garden.

The parish invites those who are homeless to their parish often, including for an annual "Pastor's Thanksgiving Dinner," in which the homeless and parishioners break bread together as one family. "GoMAD is derived from the idea that you have to get to know someone who is homeless—you have to fall in love with them—to really care about the issue," Pam says.

The six agencies St. Mary's partners with have even developed stronger relationships among themselves because of the parish's involvement, referring individuals to the other organizations based on need and available resources.

With its model based on building relationships, connecting with community partners, and involving diverse groups of parishioners, the GoMAD initiative is an exemplary outreach and charity program.

4. Advocating for Justice: Legislative Action

Sometimes, peace and justice ministry means wearing an old T-shirt and jeans and working on home construction with an agency like Habitat for Humanity. Other times, it means wearing your Sunday best to a meeting with a lawmaker's staff member about pending immigration legislation.

"Parishes can help lift up the moral and human dimension of public issues, calling people to informed participation in the political process," the bishops write in Communities of Salt and Light. "The voices of parishioners need to be heard on behalf of vulnerable children—born and unborn—on behalf of those who suffer discrimination and injustice, on behalf of those without health care or housing, on behalf of our land and water, our communities and neighborhoods." Legislative action—lobbying those in power to make decisions that lift up those on the margins—is one of the least understood, most potentially controversial areas of peace and justice ministry. It is also one of the most important. Think back to the story of Archbishop Oscar Romero in the "Rights and Responsibilities" section of the last chapter. The primary way he practiced justice was to use his voice to speak truth to power. When we promote peace and justice through interactions with legislators, we live Romero's legacy.

Too often, our church has not been great at helping Catholics understand the importance of faith-based political engagement. Here are a few concerns peace and justice leaders might hear when inviting parishioners to participate in legislative action, and some ways to respond to those concerns.

Concern: The church shouldn't be getting into politics. What about the separation of church and state?

Response: "The separation of church and state" means that our government cannot sponsor or block the practice of any religion. It *does not* mean that people of faith cannot bring their values to the public square. Our First Amendment right to free speech means that all individuals and organizations, regardless of faith, are able to do so. As politics are the way important decisions are made that affect the common good, people and organizations of faith are called on to participate in the conversation through legislative advocacy.

Concern: I believe what the church teaches about human life and dignity, but isn't getting involved in legislative advocacy imposing what I believe on others?

Response: While Catholic advocates get involved in public policy lobbying because of their faith, the positions the church holds on social issues are accessible to human reason. You don't have to be a Catholic to understand the argument that an undocumented immigrant is worthy of respect, for instance. "Faith helps us see more clearly the truth about human life and dignity that we also understand through human reason," the bishops write.[7] Another way to think about it: if someone believed that slavery was OK, you'd have no trouble "imposing" your belief that slavery is wrong on them, would you?

Concern: Is the church going to tell me who to vote for?

Response: No, never! While the Catholic Church raises its voice on crucial issues of the day, the church never endorses political parties, platforms, or candidates. The church teaches that a conscience well-formed by Catholic moral and social teaching should be each person's guide in the voting booth. This area of peace and justice ministry is never partisan: "As Catholics, we should be guided more by our moral convictions than by our attachment to a political party or interest group," the bishops write.[8] "In today's environment, Catholics may feel politically disenfranchised, sensing that no party and few candidates fully share our comprehensive commitment to human life and dignity." While voting is clearly an important element of political participation, it's the process of ongoing advocacy on key issues through phone calls, emails, letters, in-person visits, and public demonstrations that is what this area of peace and justice ministry is really about.

Concern: You're asking me to write my legislator about a social issue. Who decides the church's positions on particular pieces of legislation?

Response: Legislative action in Catholic communities is best done when following the lead of the US Conference of Catholic Bishops, other national Catholic organizations like Catholic Relief Services and Catholic Charities USA, and state-based Catholic conferences. These organizations employ public policy experts who apply CST to current issues and events. Then, with the endorsement of bishops, these organizations communicate their positions and priorities and encourage Catholics to take action. Two great national networks that keep an eye on important legislation are the USCCB's "Action Center" and an initiative led by the bishops and CRS called "Catholics Confront Global Poverty." You can access both online and see what issues they are currently encouraging Catholics to speak out about.

Concern: It's all futile anyway, isn't it? Politicians don't actually care what we think.

Response: One person sending an email probably won't make a big difference. But if groups get organized, and hundreds or thousands of people contact their legislators, there's a much better chance you can make an impact. Our lawmakers work for us, remember, and we have firing and hiring rights every few years! For example, a broad coalition including faith-based groups helped secure the abolition of the death penalty in New Jersey in 2007.[9] There are success stories, even if they are not as common as we would like.

Advocacy is an act of faith and hope. We might not always win, but like any peace and justice ministry, we participate because we are called to do what we can to make the world better, and political engagement is one way positive change can happen.

5. Creating Community: Organizing for Justice

Catholic faith-based community organizing happens when a parish and other local stakeholders notice a pressing social issue in their community and come together to address it. "Many parishes are joining with other churches and groups to rebuild a sense of community in their own neighborhoods and towns," the US bishops write in Communities of Salt and Light. "These kind of church-based and community organizations are making a difference on housing, crime, education, and economic issues in local communities."

The Catholic Campaign for Human Development (CCHD) is the US Catholic Church's domestic antipoverty program that supports faith-based community organizing, inspired by the belief that those who are mostly directly affected by unjust social systems are the best people to change them. "CCHD works to break the cycle of poverty by helping low-income people participate in decisions that affect their lives, families and communities. CCHD offers a hand up, not a hand out."[10] The following is a great example of a parish working to offer a hand up to individuals in their area.

Parish Spotlight: Organizing for Justice

Parish name: Church of Our Lady of the Rosary

Location: Port Chester, New York

Initiative: Don Bosco Community Center; Don Bosco Workers, Inc.; Caritas of Port Chester

President of Don Bosco Community Center: Ann Heekin, PhD

"In 2012, Our Lady of the Rosary concluded that to meet the growing needs for social services among the Latino immigrant community in Port Chester, they would restructure parish social ministry programs as separate not-for-profits," Ann Heekin writes.

Two new organizations were created, in addition to the already-running Don Bosco Community Center: Don Bosco Workers, Inc., to serve the large immigrant day laborer population; and Caritas of Port Chester, to direct the soup kitchen, food pantry, clothing distribution, English as a second language (ESL) instruction, and emergency services.

"The three agencies at Our Lady of the Rosary provide a virtual 'city block of social services,'" Ann writes. "By developing expertise in their area of service, each group can better serve the needs of the poor while empowering them to be their own advocates for social change through access to education, food security and economic justice."

Ann describes a little bit about the work of each of the three organizations:[11]

Don Bosco Community Center's launch of a state-of-the-art technology center is the latest evolution of its mission to serve the needs of poor youth and their families through education as the path out of poverty. Computer literacy will improve college access for youth and career readiness for adults. In addition, DBCC offers a satellite course at the middle school. "Girls in Tech" is aimed at reversing the gender imbalance in technology with a girls' after-school coding club. Don Bosco is also an affiliate agency of Catholic Charities of New York.

Caritas of Port Chester (www.caritasofportchester.org) meets the growing needs of the hungry, the homeless, and the elderly in an environment that dignifies every person as a child of God. Operating six days a week, Monday–Saturday, more than 43,000 meals were served in 2013, and nearly 8,000 bags of groceries distributed by the food pantry. Also in 2013, the Open Closet clothing program served another 6,000 households. Access to ESL instruction and Emergency Assistance for medication and domestic issues round out the social services at Caritas. As a member of the Food Bank for Westchester, Caritas is also engaged in advocating for food security social policy reforms at the county level.

Don Bosco Workers (www.donboscoworkers.org) represents 200 men and women immigrant and low-skill workers in Port Chester. A worker-led program, membership provides access to a daily hiring site, trainings, and wage theft recovery assistance. A recent wage theft case filed by DBW—representing $35,000 in stolen wages—is being prosecuted by the Office of the Attorney General of New York in the Port Chester courts. DBW's advocacy to reform wage theft includes a new public education campaign—No Pay No Way: Wage Theft Is Bad for Port Chester—to build awareness with business owners and residents on wage theft's impact on the entire community. Don Bosco Workers is also active in wage theft reform at the state level with new legislation to amend New York State wage and hour law to improve restitution rates for wage claims. The Catholic Campaign for Human Development is the principal funder for Don Bosco Workers.

6. Building Solidarity: Beyond Parish Boundaries

"Catholic social teaching more than anything else insists that we are one family; it calls us to overcome barrier of race, religion, ethnicity, gender, economic status, and nationality," the bishops write in Communities of Salt and Light. "Parishes need to be bridge-builders, reminding us that we are part of a Universal Church with ties of faith and humanity to sisters and brothers all over the world."

When looking to invite parishioners into prayer, education, and action connected to international concerns, Catholic Relief Services is the place to start. The official international development and relief organization of the Catholic Church in the United States, CRS works expertly in about one hundred countries in diverse areas from agriculture to disaster relief to microfinance. They also engage US Catholics in building up international awareness.

Two of CRS's domestic staffers in the Northeast/Mid-Atlantic region, Cheryl Mrazik and Katie Kernich, wrote a great column for my diocesan blog, "Five Tips for Building Global Solidarity at Your Parish." They give better insight into this dimension of peace and justice ministry than I ever could, so here is an adapted version of their piece.

Five Tips for Building Global Solidarity at Your Parish[12]
By Cheryl Mrazik and Katie Kernich
1. Include the 6 o'clock news in your prayers at Mass. Often, we can feel very overwhelmed by the various conflicts, natural disasters, and other "bad news" around the world. It is easy to feel helpless and removed from these situations. But as Catholics, we are called to pray for and take action to assist those in need both in our own local communities and in our global community.

Consider relating one intercession during the prayers of the faithful each week to a global issue that has been in the news lately. CRS often has intercessions available on their website.

2. *Create a visible reminder of your parish's commitment to our brothers and sisters around the world.* Your parish could start a chalice program, through which individuals or families in the parish can sign up to take a chalice home for a week and spend that week praying for people in another part of the world. Your parish might also display a "world prayer map" on which parishioners can place pins to indicate people or parts of our country and the world for which they are praying, inviting the rest of the parish community to join with them in prayer.

3. *Invite speakers to your parish who address global issues.* Many parishes have missions during Advent or Lent that include speakers. This would be an opportune time to invite a speaker who can share with the parish community about a particular global issue, or about the church around the world. Many Catholic religious orders with missions overseas have speakers available for parishes. You may also invite a parishioner or someone else from the local community who has immigrated to the US to share stories from his or her home country. CRS Global Fellows are priests and deacons available throughout the year, at no cost to the parish, to speak at parish masses about the global work of the church and CRS's projects overseas.

4. *Celebrate members of your parish community who are living out our call to global solidarity.* In your parish bulletin once a month, spotlight a parishioner or group of parishioners who has volunteered, advocated, or shown other types of support for global solidarity. At Mass, have the parish community bless parishioners who are traveling on mission trips overseas. When members return from trips, invite them to share their experiences in some way with the rest of the parish.

5. *Commit as a community to a particular global issue.* Many Catholic parishes "twin" with other parishes overseas. Consider "twinning" as a parish for a certain period of time with a specific global issue. Select an issue theme and then try to consistently

include that theme in the life of the parish through liturgy, faith formation, community activities and events, and so forth. Create a parish prayer related to the issue, place prayer cards in the pews, and pray the prayer together at every Mass. Hunger is one issue example that has both local and global implications. Your parish could also take action to address hunger locally by serving food monthly at an antihunger organization in your community, and could address global hunger by participating in CRS Rice Bowl during Lent.

4

A Four-Step Process for Integrating Peace and Justice Ministry into Parish Life

After powerful experiences leading high school students on mission trips during my college summers, I felt called to pursue ministry as a career. So, after commencement, I ended up at the University of Notre Dame's Echo Program, which combines graduate studies in theology with two years of parish catechetical ministry and community living. Two classmates and I were assigned to the Archdiocese of Milwaukee, where we each had our own parish.

Bright-eyed and bushy-tailed, I decided I was going to light my whole affluent, suburban parish on fire with my passion for Catholic social teaching (CST) and peace and justice ministry within a month or two.

This did not happen, of course. I had no idea how a parish worked.

But I am an optimistic believer in the G.K. Chesterton quote, "If a thing is worth doing, it is worth doing badly."[1] There are always a lot of things to learn from failure. So here are three lessons from my unsuccessful attempts to turn a parish into a bastion of peace and justice activity overnight.

1. Most Catholics Are Not Familiar with Catholic Social Teaching

In my current job, parishes sometimes invite me to give a talk on CST to a gathering of adults. I often take an informal poll, asking people to raise their hand if they have heard of CST. On average, about one in five folks raise their hands—and these groups are typically composed of disciples who are interested in Catholicism enough to come to an optional adult faith formation event. The Catholic bishops of the United States recognize this challenging fact in Communities of Salt and Light: "For too many parishioners, our social teaching is an unknown tradition," they write.

In their landmark book *Catholic Social Teaching: Our Best Kept Secret*, authors Edward DeBerri and James Hug suggest a few reasons why CST remains "secret": the core documents seem abstract and are not easy to read; the topics addressed in CST are controversial social issues and can make people uncomfortable; and, in general, authoritative church statements are less attractive today than authentic witness.[2]

For these reasons and others, we often haven't done the best job as a church at handing on CST. I didn't realize this at first at my parish in Wisconsin, and I grew frustrated when my excitement was met with confusion or blank stares. I acted out of this frustration whenever I had the chance to speak in front of a group at the parish. My motto was the famous quote from the late-nineteenth-century humorist Finley Peter Dunne: "Comfort the afflicted and afflict the comfortable." I particularly relished the latter half of this expression and used any chance I had to share grim statistics about child mortality, say, around the world. This barrage made people feel bad about themselves, but it surely didn't inspire conversion. My zeal was a turnoff. I'm sure some people saw me as a naïve, radical activist to be ignored.

My perspective needed a readjustment. Instead of looking at the widespread lack of familiarity with CST as a roadblock to building peace and justice ministry at the parish, coworkers on the parish staff helped me to see it as a privileged opportunity for faith formation. And difficult concepts and statistics are not good starting points for faith formation. I learned that when working to pass on CST . . .

2. There Is No Substitute for Firsthand Experience

I reflected on my own story. What experiences sparked my passion? What led me to parish ministry? Not reading a book or hearing a talk. This sort of learning was essential, but it didn't come first. Instead, what kick-started my commitment to peace and justice were face-to-face interactions with people living on the margins of society, and then reflection on how I had seen the face of Christ in those individuals.

I had watched a similar conversion occur in a high school student the summer I discovered my call to work in peace and justice ministry, just a few years before. The class clown and freshman team quarterback with a Ronald McDonald-style helmet of brown hair, Connor, was in the small group of students I chaperoned on a weeklong, faith-based summer service immersion program called JusticeworX. We spent our week with young children at a Catholic nursery school in an impoverished inner city. Unfairly, I didn't expect much from Connor at first, who didn't seem that interested in or knowledgeable about his faith. But he was incredible with the three-year-olds, assuming the roles of human jungle gym, playground monster, and gifted storyteller with gusto. He fell in love with the kids.

One afternoon, one of the children acted out violently, punching and biting others in the class. Repeated time-outs didn't work. "What's going on, big guy?" Connor asked, with anger and exasperation in his voice. A teacher in the class came over to us. "I just called his dad to come pick him up," she said. "He was just released from jail this morning." We fell immediately silent, and Connor's eyes widened.

That night, back at the retreat center where we were staying, we talked about the challenges people face all over the world, just because of where they happen to be born. For instance, according to the World Health Organization, life expectancy in the United States is about eighty years, but it's only forty-six in the African nation of Sierra Leone.[3] We reflected on how this cannot be God's dream for the world, who creates all people and loves them equally. Wheels started turning in Connor's head. The next day, during our group's lunch break at the nursery school, Connor began to pace back and forth. "When we go back to school, we just have to do something," he said. One of the other students found a pen and started taking notes on a napkin. They talked about lunch in the cafeteria at school, and how their classmates often had some change left over after buying a meal or snack. "What if we asked people just to chip in a few cents every day?" one student proposed. "We could call it 'Dime-a-Day.'"

They brought the idea to their other classmates on the trip, and they met up later that summer to plan. After getting approval from their high school administration, they had T-shirts made and painted globes on piggy banks. They decided to donate the money they raised to their diocese's sister diocese in Guatemala, where some would help women start small businesses and the rest would go toward building a water tower. In their first few months, they raised $4,000. Connor visited the diocese in Guatemala where the funds were sent, and the Guatemalan bishop visited Connor's school to thank them.

As word spread about the project, local media covered the story. Reflecting on the start of the project, Connor told a reporter, "We had just participated in a workshop on world hunger and while I was trying to fall asleep, I thought about the presentation on world hunger and poverty. It made me really disappointed with what was happening in the world. So I thought I could make a slight change."

The workshop provided Connor with new global awareness, but it was his relationship with the local nursery-school kids that first pricked his conscience about injustice in the world, and where he had first seen Christ "in his most distressing disguise."

It was through watching the Spirit move Connor in such an awesome way that I heard the call to a career of facilitating these experiences of encounter on society's margins. How could I do that effectively within a parish context? I decided to . . .

3. Focus on Subcommunities

My initial, abstract idea about engaging the whole Wisconsin parish in some form of peace and justice ministry was way off-base. I wanted to energize the parish as a whole, but a parish doesn't exist as a monolithic entity. Faith communities are diverse in so many ways, and demand a corresponding breadth of strategies and activities. Parishioners have an extremely wide assortment of opinions, experiences, and backgrounds. We are at various life stages and participate in the community at varying levels. James Joyce's definition of Catholicism—"Here comes everybody"—is right on the money. No single approach is going to engage everyone.

I think I knew this deep down somewhere, but I still spent a lot of time thinking and talking about the parish in broad, sweeping terms. It is valuable to know a parish's dominant culture, but any sort of cultural change like the one I was hoping for happens one small group at a time. Connor's transformation happened within a small group of his peers, after all.

For the rest of my time in Wisconsin, and as a parish youth minister and diocesan worker in the years since, I have approached each parish as a "community of communities," and focused on specific cohorts of parishioners—a small faith community of adults, a religious education class of fifth graders, high school seniors preparing for college, and so on. With each group, I try to work with others to replicate the process that had worked so well for Connor.

Discern, Act, Reflect, Transform

The Catholic Diocese of Richmond, Virginia's Office of Social Ministries developed the fabulous "DART Method of Social

Ministry," modeled after the classic Catholic "See-Judge-Act" process pioneered by Fr. Joseph Cardijn in the early twentieth century. DART is an acronym that stands for:

Discern community needs and Parish resources.

Act to meet the immediate needs of your community.

Reflect on your experience in light of the Gospel and CST.

Transform social structures to achieve the common good.[4]

It's a helpful schema that nicely outlines the arc of Connor's conversion, and it can be applied in virtually any pastoral setting, with care taken to construct experiences in age-appropriate ways. Starting with these steps is a great way to make room for the Holy Spirit to form disciples committed to peace and justice who might never have heard of CST before.

This section of the chapter is primarily intended for ecclesial ministers who already serve in various capacities at the parish level: parish catechetical leaders and DREs, pastors and pastoral associates, youth ministers, peace and justice committee leaders, RCIA team members, sacrament prep coordinators, liturgists, and so on. As you read about DART, keep the subcommunity or communities you work with in mind. Where might there be opportunities to use the method within what you already have going on?

The call for this sort of integration comes straight from Communities of Salt and Light. The bishops write, "We need to build local communities of faith where our social teaching is central, not fringe; where social ministry is integral, not optional; where it is the work of every believer, not just the mission of a few committed people and committees. . . . The parishes that are leaders in this area see social ministry not as a specialized ministry, but as an integral part of the entire parish. They weave the Catholic social mission into every aspect of parish life—worship, formation, and action. They follow a strategy of integration and collaboration, which keeps social ministry from becoming isolated or neglected."

How can our parishes avoid leaving social ministry to just a few people or a single committee? One key way is to "weave the Catholic social mission into every aspect of parish life," the bishops write. So the rest of this chapter is not about starting brand-new initiatives. Instead, it will focus on making peace and justice activity a key component of parish activities that are already happening.

First, I'll walk through the four steps of DART, showing how they are exemplified in Connor's story and in some other ministry experiences. Then, I'll suggest some practical ways that parish leaders can integrate the DART process into particular programs.

Discern Community Needs and Parish Resources

The authors of DART begin with community discernment. This two-part process involves *looking out* at the world around you and *looking in* at the talents and resources of your faith community.

First, look outward: What are the needs in your local community or surrounding areas? Is hunger an issue? The arrival of immigrants? Lack of affordable housing? Violence? A good way to learn about the needs around your community is to contact agencies and organizations that are working to meet these needs. Many of these organizations depend on volunteer support, which will come into play in the Act phase of DART. In particular, see if you can find an organization that facilitates face-to-face interactions with individuals who are living on society's margins. Pope Francis's "Culture of Encounter" requires this sort of in-person experience. There are two other big advantages to partnering with agencies outside the parish: you don't have to reinvent the wheel and try to launch a social service agency yourself, and organizations accustomed to working with volunteers can handle any safety or logistical concerns that might come up.

Spend time building a relationship with at least one of these agencies that your faith community hasn't connected with before. Over a meal with someone who works for the organization you've connected with, learn about what they do and ask how the parish might support their work.

As you're building these relationships, also gather with other parish leaders interested in peace and justice ministry and look inward. What talents do your parishioners possess? What sub-communities in the parish might be ready to take action? How would a peace and justice initiative fit into the parish schedule or help fulfill parish goals and priorities?

In Connor's case, the discernment step was done by the JusticeworX program and its parent nonprofit organization, the Center for FaithJustice. The Center partners with a wide variety of community agencies in and around its home city of Trenton, New Jersey. The nursery school and day camp where Connor served liked to have high school-age volunteers spend time with their students, as the high schoolers are usually good role models for the little ones.

A parish-based discernment step that worked well during my high school youth ministry work happened when my pastor mentioned that he said Mass at a local nursing home once a month, and invited me to bring a group of students to the home for the liturgy and some fellowship. The community need my pastor noticed was the loneliness present for many residents of the home, and he figured our parish's youth would bring some energy and fun to the space. It was a perfect match, as the four or five teenagers who came each time loved spending time with the seniors and listening to their stories.

Act to Meet the Immediate Needs of Your Community

Once you've discerned some of the needs in your community and the ability of a group within the parish to respond, the next step is to act. The action step is where the work of building a culture of encounter really gets going. And most often, encounter with those who are often ignored or forgotten means getting off the parish property! This is where partnership with community organizations is crucial. Their expertise and infrastructure are essential resources. "Going it alone," even with the best intentions, isn't prudent.

The action piece of Connor's conversion was his time spent with the nursery-school children. One key element of his experience was the fact that his relationships with the children were given space to grow: he spent six or seven hours with them five days in a row. He got to know the kids' names, their stories, and their personalities, and he shared his own with them. Such an intensive period of encounter might not be feasible for you, but the action step is not a one-shot deal. It takes time and some measure of regularity to help relationships across social barriers develop.

Before the action step begins for the subcommunity you're working with, highlight the importance of this sort of relationship. Invite your group to learn the names of the people they meet and something about them. With an emphasis on kinship, as opposed to "helping," you can work to keep any sort of "savior complex" out of the equation. Too often in the action piece of social ministry, we set it up as a one-way transaction: a "more fortunate" person generously gives to a "less fortunate" person. This misses the point of encounter. As all people are created in the image and likeness of God, we are all equal in his eyes. It's important to frame action steps this way.

One community organization that builds this type of kinship beautifully is the St. Ben's Community Meal in Milwaukee. While groups from churches and other places serve the meal each evening, which is primarily for those living in poverty in the city, other groups are invited to come to eat and spend time with the patrons. I went with a group of adults from my Wisconsin parish to share in the meal one night, and it was powerful to watch the experience change all of us. We're so used to serving and fixing, and there was some strong, initial discomfort with being served. But the fellowship around the same table, which reached across social boundaries, helped us see our neighbors living in poverty in a new way. We weren't solving a problem, but building companionship.

Processing an experience of encounter like the St. Ben's meal or Connor's time with the nursery-school students is vital, and it's the third step in the DART Method.

Reflect on Your Experience in the Light of the Gospel and CST

In his masterpiece *Four Quartets*, poet T. S. Eliot writes, "We had the experience but missed the meaning."[5] How easy it is to let experiences pass us by without reflecting on them and inviting them to change us. A mentor of mine in peace and justice ministry, the creator of the JusteworX program that transformed Connor, is direct about the centrality of reflection: "If you take action and don't reflect on it, the action was a waste of time," he says.

Setting aside time for reflection immediately after the action is completed can be a challenge. It requires asking for a longer time commitment from those who participate in the action. It might mean cutting the moment of encounter a bit short to make time for reflection. No matter what it takes, be sure to plan for it.

Reflection is done best in groups small enough to allow all to contribute; the six-to-ten range is usually good. If you're working with a larger group, you might want to split up into smaller circles for reflection, making sure each group is led by a prepared leader.

Preparing to be a small-group discussion leader ahead of time is important, especially since the difficult social issues at play in your group's experience might come up and lead to disagreement and tension. You'll want to prepare yourself and other discussion leaders for this in two primary ways: do some background research ahead of time and make a list of small-group discussion best practices (and then stick to the list!).

There are scores of helpful resources available that outline the church's teachings on difficult issues. You don't have to be an expert, but some basic reading can help you provide good background information on social questions. On immigration issues, for instance, the US Conference of Catholic Bishops' Justice for Immigrants campaign (www.justiceforimmigrants.org)

provides a helpful list of common myths about immigration and the church's responses. Google is a powerful tool, but it's best to use it to find official church websites and documents.

There are some great books on CST you might want to add to your library as well. I recommend *Living Justice: Catholic Social Teaching in Action* by Thomas Massaro, SJ, and *The Challenge and Spirituality of Catholic Social Teaching* by Marvin L. Krier Mich.

In terms of the actual content of the discussion time, there are three important types of reflection that should all be included after an experience of encounter on the society's margins: sensory, social, and theological reflection.

Sensory reflection is the first step, and it focuses on a recap of what happened during the experience. Ask participants to summarize the encounter—not only what happened externally, but what happened to them internally. Provide some questions written on paper, give a few minutes for quiet reflection, and then begin the conversation. Try questions like these:

- What did you notice going on around you?

- What surprised you or inspired you?

- What was the most difficult part of the experience?

- Did you meet someone who you'll carry in your heart? What was that person's name, and what did you learn about him or her?

- What moment from the experience will you remember for a long time?

Social reflection includes the big "Why?" questions. It encourages participants to get to the root of the social issue(s) they experienced. Here are some example social reflection questions:

- Why do you think the social issue we encountered exists?

- How are people's lives affected by this situation? Who benefits? Who suffers?

- What people, institutions, and values contribute to this situation? Who might be involved in potential solutions?
- What obstacles exist for people who might be trying to overcome this situation?
- What other social issues are connected to this one we encountered?
- What are people who are most affected about this situation saying about it?

There are no easy answers to these questions. The goal here is to introduce complexity and to dig a little deeper into pressing social issues that we might usually leave underexplored. If things like poverty and homelessness are not consistent with God's dream for the world, it's incumbent on disciples to grapple with the problems and ask "Why?" In his World Day of Peace Message in 1985, Pope St. John Paul II emphasized this idea: "We should not limit ourselves to deploring the negative effects of the present situation of crisis and injustice," he wrote. "What we are really required to do is destroy the roots that cause these effects."

Theological reflection puts our experience in dialogue with our faith. We are not called to work for peace and justice because it seems like a nice thing to do. We are called because it is a central part of our faith tradition. The values of volunteerism and "giving back" are everywhere today. Theological reflection helps us to bring the richness of CST to these secular values: we are more than "volunteers" when we build a culture of encounter. We are disciples of Christ. Here are some theological reflection questions:

- Where is God at work here? Did you see the face of Christ anywhere?
- Is there a passage from Scripture this makes you think of?
- Do you see any connection between this and the Eucharist?

- What beliefs and values lead you to say, "Things shouldn't be this way"?
- Can you think of any relevant stories or words from the life of a saint?
- How do you think Jesus would respond to this situation?
- Was there love here? Hope? Faith?
- As disciples, we are called by God to do his work in the world. How did this experience affect your sense of calling? How will your discipleship be different after today?

As part of the group's theological reflection, you might want to select a relevant Scripture passage or quote from CST that connects to their experience.

Connor's week at JusticeworX was full of all three types of reflection. Each morning of the week, an interactive prayer service with Scripture, ritual action, song, and spoken prayer framed the day of encounter to come in theological terms. At lunchtime, our group would recap what had happened that morning, and then, in the evenings, we would split up and meet with participants from other service groups on the trip, sharing experiences with one another. Other evening activities, like the presentation on poverty around the world that really hit Connor hard, helped the students do some social reflection. Before going to bed each night, participants were invited to take part in an Ignatian-style *examen* prayer called "gifts and challenges," when they would share where they had encountered God in two key moments from the day. All of these forms of reflection work together to assure that participants did not miss the meaning of their experience.

Transform Social Structures to Achieve the Common Good

The reflection after the action is meant to lead to some big changes. To keep the momentum going after a positive experience, there has to be a "next step." How will life be different after this shared encounter? How will our community be different? How might the *world* be different?

While the most recent iteration of DART Method focuses primarily on the transformation of social structures, older resources from the Diocese of Richmond also highlight what it calls personal transformation and interpersonal transformation.

Personal transformation means that the action and reflection experience lead the participant to change some things about his or her daily life. Ask, "What comes next for you because of this experience?" Someone who ate at St. Ben's Community Meal in Milwaukee, for instance, might commit to wasting less food, donating money to the organization, and visiting the people she met back at the meal once every few weeks. Connor's decision to devote a huge amount of time to getting "Dime-a-Day" off the ground represented his own personal transformation.

Interpersonal transformation means getting other members of the community involved, allowing one's own personal change to reach out to others. Dime-a-Day was not something just Connor and a couple of his friends did. They brought the project to their entire school community. Back in Wisconsin, the group that ate at St. Ben's might organize a hygiene products drive at their parish for the patrons there, and then invite a new group of parishioners to deliver the items and stay for a meal. Excitement from fellow parishioners about a certain peace and justice initiative is the most effective way of engaging others within the faith community.

Structural transformation means working to change the systems that lead to social injustices. Moving beyond meeting the immediate needs of individuals, structural transformation focuses on long-term, community-based solutions. (Recall the differences between charity and justice, outlined in chap. 2.) The money Dime-a-Day raised supported women who wanted to start their own businesses—a hand-up more than a hand-out. Such investment has the ability to invigorate a local community's economy. The St. Ben's meal group might organize a letter-writing campaign to urge elected leaders to pass legislation that helps lift up those who are living in poverty.

The DART process never ends. Hopefully, transformed disciples are led to another moment of discernment, and the cycle continues.

DARTing with Specific Subcommunities in a Parish

The DART Method can be applied generally for any parish group, but it can have an even bigger impact if you use it creatively with your specific subcommunity in mind. What topics and themes are central to your particular ministry, and how might those themes have a connection to the ministry of peace and justice? If you have a captive audience, how can you capitalize on that opportunity without asking them for more time? Here is one example of subcommunity-specific DARTing to get your mind going.

Subcommunity: Recently Confirmed Students or Those Preparing for the Sacrament

Main theme: The Gifts of the Holy Spirit

Peace and Justice Connection: The Gifts of the Holy Spirit help us to notice and take action when there is something wrong in the world that is not consistent with God's love for all people, like poverty or hunger. Four examples:

- *Reverence* for God and all his creation inspires us to have care for all people.
- *Wisdom* helps us to realize that something like hunger is not part of God's dream for the world.
- *Right judgment* helps us to evaluate the situation and choose to do what is right.
- *Courage* gives us the strength to act when it would be easier to do nothing.

Discern:
- As an at-home assignment or in an in-person session, invite students to learn about organizations in or around their

community that help lift up those who are suffering. Discuss findings and choose an organization to connect with.

Act:
- Volunteer at the organization during a scheduled class session. If impossible, invite someone from the organization to come to the class and talk about what they do. Or, participate in an in-seat project that supports the organization (e.g., sandwich making for a soup kitchen).

Reflect:
- Sensory: What part of the experience was most powerful for you? Who is someone you met through the experience, and what will you remember about him or her?
- Social: What things impressed you the most about the organization? Why do you think there are people who have to go to this organization for support?
- Theological: What gift of the Holy Spirit was most important to this project? Why? In the Bible, Jesus tells his disciples to love God with all their strength and their neighbor as themselves. What are some ways we can show love to God and neighbor as confirmed disciples?

Transform:
- Invite participants to commit to one thing they can do to continue the work of justice in the month ahead. Have participants write their commitment on an index card, and then display the cards in the form of a cross—a reminder that the work of compassion is Jesus' work in the world.

5

The Roles of a Peace and Justice Coordinating Committee

In his great book *My Lord & My God: Engaging Catholics in Social Ministry*, Jeffry Odell Korgen tells the story of a social action director in an archdiocese who visits a parish and asks the pastor if the community has a social concerns committee. "Oh, you mean Bertha! Bertha's great. She would be a big help to you! I don't know what I'd do without Bertha!" Korgen writes, "Bertha? She *was* the social concerns committee! Perhaps when the Last Judgment of Matthew 25 occurs, Bertha will join a select flock of sheep in heaven. Her lonely toil will ultimately be rewarded. And she will say to the goats, 'I gave you many opportunities to feed Jesus, but you did not read the bulletin. I offered you a chance to give Jesus a drink, but you did not listen to the announcements. Depart from me, you accursed, into the fire prepared for the devil and his angels!' . . . Rule #1: Don't be a Bertha."[1]

This chapter is meant to help you follow Korgen's first rule. To effectively engage an entire faith community in peace and justice ministry, a robust committee of committed parishioners is needed. I'll break down the chapter into three specific phases: (1) creating or renewing a peace and justice coordinating committee; (2) planning and executing activities; (3) looking ahead.

Phase 1: Creating or Renewing a Peace and Justice Coordinating Committee

This section will look at the first steps in forming or rejuvenating a peace and justice coordinating committee by examining these topics: purpose of the committee; connecting with parish leadership; member recruitment; the committee's first months.

Purpose of the Committee

The purpose of a peace and justice coordinating committee is revealed in this name itself.

Peace and Justice: This phrase simply states the area of this ministry, and uses very similar language to the Vatican's unit that works on these issues (which is called the Pontifical Council for Justice and Peace). The range of Catholic social teaching (CST) topics and activity areas that comprise peace and justice ministry are covered in chapters 2 and 3, respectively.

Coordinating: This word is a reminder that these parish groups will not do peace and justice ministry on behalf of the parish, but will organize experiences for others to participate in. In other words, these groups are not just collections of Berthas, but are strategic planners and conveners.

Committee: The standard name for a group that gathers with a particular mission.

One note about what the purpose of these committees is *not*: they are not meant to *replace* already existent outreach initiatives or groups, but to *network* and *supplement* them.

For instance, Society of St. Vincent de Paul conferences are common organizers of charitable outreach in Catholic parishes. But as the areas of peace and justice ministry enumerated in Communities of Salt and Light extend beyond the scope and mission of St. Vincent de Paul, other forms of activity are also needed. Also, as a networking body, it would be smart for a PJCC at a parish with already existent groups like St. Vincent de Paul to invite a representative or two to serve on the committee so the parish can be unified in its efforts.

Connecting with Parish Leadership

Before moving ahead with the formation of a PJCC, or when looking to expand your participants or reform an already-existent committee, it's imperative to connect with the pastor and other leaders in the parish. Request a meeting with the pastor to outline your ideas and get his input. A basic level of support from the pastor is necessary, and, if peace and justice ministry is of particular interest to him, his deeper involvement could help the PJCC have a broader, faster impact on the whole parish.

After securing support from the pastor, it's smart to connect with other parish leaders, depending on the structure of your own faith community. Pastoral associates, deacons, directors of religious education, youth ministers, and other pastoral leaders can all be helpful animators of peace and justice ministry in the parish. In the two most successful PJCCs that have started recently in the diocese where I work, each had a pastor or pastoral associate actually serve on the committee and attend meetings. This type of connection is helpful for several reasons:

These leaders should have a good grasp on the culture and calendar of the parish, helping the PJCC coordinate activities that fit in well with the overall mission of the community.

Leaders who are involved in different ministries can be "peace and justice emissaries" to those ministries, which will help infuse CST into all areas of parish life.

Practically speaking, parish staff can help the PJCC schedule for parish space and get the word out about its activities.

Member Recruitment

With the support of parish leadership, it's time to start recruiting members to serve on the PJCC. In addition to one or more parish staff members, if possible, you'll want to build a team of about eight to twelve total volunteers. Jeff Bezos, founder of Amazon .com, calls this the "two pizza rule": you never want to have a meeting at which two pizzas couldn't feed the entire group.[2]

The most effective tool in recruiting volunteers to join the PJCC (or any ministry) is personal invitation. Widespread announcements in the bulletin or online are fine, but it's rare you'll get significant turnout for committee service that way. Instead, those leading the committee's formation should brainstorm a diverse list of parishioners who would be good fits. Some questions for reflection as you build this initial list:

- Who do I know who has a heart for those who are poor and vulnerable?
- Who are newer parishioners not involved in much yet who might be interested in contributing to this particular ministry?
- What peace and justice activities has our parish participated in in the past, and who was involved in those?
- Who has a special skill or profession that he or she might be able to use in this ministry?
- Do we have people of diverse ages, backgrounds, and ministry experience levels on the list?

In *My Lord & My God*, Jeff Korgen emphasizes that you're not looking for "joiners," or those who will show up because they read something in the bulletin. You're looking for leaders—those people who can bring others into the social justice mission of the parish. Qualities of good leaders, Korgen writes, include "listening skills, communication skills, healthy anger, sense of humor, spirituality, awareness of death, and most important 'has followers'" (23).

Once you have a preliminary list of invitees, approach each one individually with a phone call or handwritten note. Meet for coffee and learn about their faith journey and their particular gifts and talents. If he or she seems interested in serving on the committee, ask him or her for a six-meeting commitment, after which he or she can evaluate further participation. (The first six sessions of a nascent PJCC are outlined in chap. 6, and will be discussed briefly in the next section.)

If you're struggling to come up with a list of potential leaders, an approach that works occasionally is to have a one-time justice-themed event. As the life and justice director for my diocese, parishes hoping to start a PJCC have invited me to give talks on various social justice topics. Those parishes collect attendees' information and follow up with them one-on-one about the PJCC. Your own diocesan social justice office or Catholic Charities agency should be able to provide or recommend a good local guest speaker.

The Committee's First Months

Once you have a two-pizza-sized committee that has agreed to attend six meetings, consider using the sessions laid out in chapter 6. These six 60–75 minute sessions provide an introduction to CST; cover the six areas of peace and justice ministry; invite the committee to name itself and develop a mission statement; introduce the Discern, Act, Reflect, Transform process (as described in chap. 4); and guide the group in beginning to plan activities for the parish to participate in. They're suitable sessions for brand-new committees or already-existent ones that are looking to deepen their commitment or spark some new energy.

In addition to these six meetings, consider inviting the group to participate in team-building activities together, such as sharing a potluck meal or serving together in partnership with a local community organization. One reformed PJCC I've worked with served as volunteers at a local homeless shelter together. Then, in the following months, one or two PJCC members would lead other parishioners on visits to the shelter. A partnership between the shelter and parish has developed, emerging from that first visit as a team.

The first few months of the PJCC's existence—even up to a year—are more about learning, team building, and laying groundwork than they are about planning and executing. Without a solid background in CST, understanding the areas of peace and justice ministry, and focusing on group cohesion, it will be hard for the PJCC to be successful.

Phase 2: Planning and Executing Activities

This section will cover five practical concerns a PJCC will want to keep in mind when planning and executing activities: (A) vary the activities you plan by length, area of peace and justice ministry, and CST theme; (B) connect with national initiatives; (C) for everything, there is a season; (D) build bridges with other parish ministries; (E) get the word out.

A. Vary the Activities You Plan by Length, Area of Peace and Justice Ministry, and CST Theme

Variety is the spice of life, and of peace and justice ministry. Pat Slater, pastoral associate for justice and community outreach at the Catholic Community of Christ Our Light in Cherry Hill, New Jersey, recommends coordinating events that attract both "marathoners" and "sprinters." In the busyness of life, however, most people are most likely to participate in something designed for sprinters. "Periodically, the parish puts out a stewardship sheet with opportunities for short-term commitments like taking a turn at our community food pantry or helping with driving our Guatemala Mission team to the airport," Pat says. "We also have sandwich making once a month on a Sunday morning which is a great hit with families, especially ones with small children."[3]

Also, as you look to plan some initial activities, you'll want to have a variety of areas of peace and justice ministry and CST themes covered. A brand-new PJCC at Blessed Teresa of Calcutta Parish in Collingswood and Westmont, New Jersey, decided to introduce itself to the community with a diverse five-week series of activities addressing the conditions Jesus describes in the Last Judgment story in Matthew 25:31-46. In the weeks leading up to the Feast of Christ the King, which includes the Last Judgment gospel once every three years, the PJCC coordinated what they called "The Matthew 25 Project." The initiative included these activities:

Week 1: I was hungry and you fed me, thirsty and you gave me drink.
   Activity: Two nights of sandwich making for local food relief organizations, including one night designed for religious education families and one night led by the parish's Society of St. Vincent de Paul conference.

   Areas of peace and justice ministry: outreach and charity; education

   Themes of CST: call to community; call to family; rights and responsibilities; option for the poor

Week 2: I was a stranger and you welcomed me.
   Activity: Panel discussion of three local residents who immigrated to the US from Iraq, Liberia, and Mexico. Two of the speakers worked with the local Catholic Charities refugee resettlement program, and the third participated in a parish's immigration reform efforts. Attendees were invited to sign postcards to their legislators advocating for comprehensive immigration reform.

   Areas of peace and justice ministry: education; legislative action; building solidarity

   Themes of CST: solidarity; call to participation

Week 3: I was naked and you clothed me.
   Activity: Parishioners were asked to cook casseroles for a local homeless shelter. Two small groups of parishioners visited the shelter this week to serve dinner and spend time with the guests there.

   Area of peace and justice ministry: outreach and charity

   Themes of CST: life and dignity of the human person; option for the poor and vulnerable

Week 4: I was ill and you cared for me.
   Activity: Communal anointing of the sick featuring a reflection from a nurse who serves in the parish nurses association.

Areas of peace and justice ministry: prayer and worship; education

Themes of CST: life and dignity of the human person; call to community

Week 5: I was in prison and you visited me.
Activity: Diocese's coordinator of prison ministry shared a reflection on prison ministry with the group in the context of a faith-sharing session on the Matthew 25 gospel passage.

Areas of peace and justice ministry: prayer and worship; education

Themes of CST: life and dignity of the human person

Not every area of peace and justice ministry or every theme of CST was covered in this series, but the diversity of experiences introduced members of the parish to the wide range of activities that fall under the peace and justice umbrella. As an opening initiative, the Matthew 25 Project was very successful: short, clear, time-bound activities of various types encouraged widespread participation by a diverse range of parishioners.

B. Connect with National Initiatives

There's no need to reinvent the wheel when planning CST activities. There are a number of national organizations that provide great options for engaging a parish in peace and justice ministry.

St. Patrick Catholic Community in Scottsdale, Arizona, has strong partnerships with three different national organizations: JustFaith Ministries, Family Promise, and Open Table.

JustFaith Ministries (www.justfaith.org) develops transformational programs that invite participants into a deeper understanding of CST and how they are called to bring God's compassion to the world. Parishes run these programs for small groups of participants, and there's nothing better out there to ignite a passion for justice in Catholic disciples. At St. Patrick's, alumni of JustFaith programs are invited to plug into an initiative called "Beyond JustFaith," which coordinates various peace and justice initiatives for the parish. The zeal that JustFaith produces is given an outlet right away.

Family Promise (www.familypromise.org) serves and empowers homeless families. Their primary program connects families with faith communities that host families in their own buildings for a week at a time. "Parishioners are engaged by making and sharing meals, serving as overnight chaperones, and helping with evening activities for and with the families," St. Patrick's director of pastoral activities Mary Permoda says.

Open Table (www.theopentable.org) trains parishioners to accompany individuals living in poverty. Six to ten St. Patrick's parishioners walk with a brother or sister living in poverty for about a year, supporting them by helping them to create and implement an action plan.

C. For Everything, There Is a Season

Trust the wisdom of the liturgical year. Times of increased parish activity—Advent, Lent, and Easter, in particular—should have peace and justice components as well. In Lent, for instance, the season's emphasis on almsgiving is a natural connecting point. While a PJCC might be tempted to steer clear of already-busy times, these are the seasons in which people are looking for some form of engagement.

Laura Flanagan, director of religious education at Incarnate Word Parish in Chesterfield, Missouri, used Lent as a time to invite parishioners to participate in the corporal works of mercy. "As I was considering committing myself to participating in all the corporal works of mercy during Lent, I considered a way to make the parishioners more aware of the works," she says.[4] "Then I remembered that this parish is full of enthusiasm and loves rising to a challenge—why not truly challenge them all to take on the works of mercy this Lent?"

Laura developed a list of options, including multiple ways that a person might participate in each work of mercy. "At least one option in each category should be able to be accomplished by a child or a person whose mobility is restricted, and I included options for taking individual initiative, working with existing Catholic and ecumenical initiatives in the city, and with existing parish ministries active in justice and charity."

Not unlike Blessed Teresa of Calcutta Parish's Matthew 25 Project, Incarnate Word focused on a different work of mercy each week, announcing each week's work from the altar and pointing parishioners toward resources where they could learn more. A few extra parish events were added, but the bulk of the project was encouraging individuals to make the corporal works of mercy part of their Lenten practice.

"The pastor and various parishioners said that our list makes them very uncomfortable," Laura says. "It is clear that each of the options listed under each work of mercy are meaningful actions, and many can be accomplished with minimal effort, yet these actions are not something most of us do on a regular basis."

D. Build Bridges with Other Parish Ministries

What ministry groups are already up and running at the parish? How might they get involved in peace and justice activities in their own settings? Can the PJCC open up a conversation with ministry leaders from different areas to talk about integration?

Here are examples of seven different parish ministries and an example of a way each one might participate in peace and justice activities:

1. *Children's ministry:* Sandwich making night for local soup kitchen and basic education about local hunger issues.

2. *Youth ministry:* Visit to nursing home and reflection on the experience.

3. *Liturgical ministries:* Use fair trade baskets (available through Catholic Relief Services' fair trade catalog) for the weekly collection.

4. *Prayer group or Legion of Mary:* Pray "Unity in Diversity: A Scriptural Rosary" that lifts up prayers for migrants and refugees.[5]

5. *RCIA:* As part of their preparatory catechesis, have a PJCC representative speak to the group about CST and lead them on a visit to a local community organization working for justice.

6. *Adult faith formation:* Six-session small faith-sharing group on the themes of CST using Paulist Evangelization Ministries' *Faith in Action* resource.[6]

7. *Marriage prep:* Use Catholic Relief Services' resource on how to include peace and justice in a wedding celebration: www.crsfairtrade.org/wedding.

The first step in working toward integration is to build relationships with those who lead the various ministries at your parish. Different PJCC members might want to connect with other ministry leaders they know to find out more about their work and explore possibilities for connection.

E. Get the Word Out

If a peace and justice activity is planned and organized, but nobody attends, does it make a sound? Publicizing your initiatives is an essential element of the ministry. Here are some publicity tips to bear in mind:

Remember the "Rule of 7 Touches." This is a basic marketing principle that claims that a person needs to hear or see your message at least seven times before he or she might even consider responding to your call for action. Some experts think it's more like thirteen touches. Either way, it's clear that . . .

Advertising in the bulletin is not enough. Very few people will show up for something just because it's advertised in the bulletin. Put your activities in the bulletin, of course, but only after you've reached out in other ways, especially through . . .

Personal invitation. PJCC members should be asked to identify three to five people each whom they can personally invite to an activity through a face-to-face mention or phone call. An individual's excitement about an activity is contagious. A good way to invite many people personally is to . . .

Greet people after Masses with informational flyers. Don't stand behind a table in the gathering space or narthex, but mingle among the departing Mass attendees, as the presider of the Mass might. If you have access to a table, invite people to write down their name, email address, and phone number so you can follow up with them. When preparing a flyer for distribution, remember . . .

Brevity is the soul of wit. Any written communication advertising your offering should be clear, clean, concise, and visually appealing. If you're using more than two fonts on a flyer, that's too many! Avoid church jargon. Include the basics: who, what, where, when, why, how.

Social media and blast emails are helpful, but they're not silver bullets. Parishes should meet people where they are, which, for a big chunk of the day, is on the internet. But a Facebook post, event invitation, or mass email is usually not enough to inspire showing up to an in-person activity. A word about social media pages: If your parish or PJCC has its own Facebook page or other social media account, be sure to post interesting articles, images, and videos that are not merely advertising for events. One rule of thumb is to post ten interesting things for every advertisement you post, and to post about once or twice a day.

No matter how hard you try, if your day and time is inconvenient, you're in trouble. While working at a parish in Wisconsin, I carefully planned and advertised a "faith and film" event for a Monday evening. When not a single person showed up, I checked the National Football League schedule, and sure enough, the Green Bay Packers were playing a game that night. Whoops! A few weeks later, with an endorsement from the pastor at the end of every Mass, more than one hundred parishioners showed up to watch the movie.

Phase 3: Looking Ahead

Social justice is embedded in the DNA of the Catholic Community of Christ Our Light in Cherry Hill, New Jersey. After decades of doing this ministry well, their peace and justice structure provides an interesting snapshot of what could be for new PJCCs someday. The parish's social justice commission is made up of ministry leaders who each coordinate a particular justice initiative, from Fair Trade to sandwich making to a "justice for immigrants" group. Each of those ministries, in turn, has a team of dedicated volunteers that coordinates activities for the parish. Essentially, the parish has a dozen or more PJCCs that focus on particular areas.

I saw movement in this direction at Blessed Teresa of Calcutta Parish, which reformed its PJCC in late 2014 (beginning with the Matthew 25 Project) after a parish merger several years before. One member of the PJCC became the point person with the local homeless shelter they support with food donations and volunteers. Another member began to serve as the group's main contact with the parish's Society of St. Vincent de Paul chapter. A married couple on the committee headed up investigation into a parish twinning opportunity with a faith community in Peru. As the parish responded well to particular initiatives, the PJCC started to develop roots and became part of the parish culture.

Jack Jezreel, founder of JustFaith Ministries and a leading national figure in peace and justice ministry, reflects on what a parish that "organizes itself around the crescendo vision of Matthew 25" might look like. It's a beautiful vision and call to action:

> It will be a parish that has anchored everything it does in the hope and intention of forming and sending its members to feed the hungry and clothe the naked and do justice. It will be a parish that organizes all of its members into mission teams. It will be a parish that sponsors its own Catholic Worker House. It will be a parish that has dozens of people doing home visits for St. Vincent de Paul and legislative visits at their congressperson's office. It will be a parish that will have started a half dozen nonprofit organizations that address needs that were not being met. It will have its own economic development committee, will host workshops on peacemaking and nonviolence, and will have a youth ministry

that looks, appropriately, a lot like the Jesuit Volunteer Corps. It will have many stories of generosity and sacrifice and heartache and joy to tell. And it will all be celebrated around a table every Sunday. Let's get started.[7]

6

Starting or Rejuvenating
a Peace and Justice
Coordinating Committee

Six sessions of conversation, education, and planning to help your parish's peace and justice coordinating committee get moving.

Facilitator Notes

Preparing for the Process: 6–8 Weeks Before Starting

The following six sessions are designed to help a parish start or reenergize a peace and justice coordinating committee. Committees of eight to twelve members are encouraged, and will gather for 60–75 minutes six times in this process.

This introductory section of chapter 6 is meant for the primary facilitator or convener of the group. It will provide some tips for planning and executing the process.

For tips on reaching out to find eight to twelve participants, see chapter 5. Invite the participants to commit to the first six sessions, after which they will have the chance to evaluate their own participation going forward.

Please read the entirety of *The Ministry of Peace and Justice* before convening the group.

Leading the Process: Six Sessions

The bulk of each of the six sessions will be spent reading a brief reading, discussing it, and participating in an activity related to the reading.

These readings are not in the book itself, but are available as printable PDFs online at Liturgical Press's website. Please print and staple enough copies for everyone in your group before each session. Or, you can direct them to print their own by accessing the website at home.

Several of the sessions' activities require additional materials, which are printed at the top of each session. You will want to review each session at least several days before it is held and gather the required materials.

Provide personal copies of *The Ministry of Peace and Justice* for every participant, as each session has readings and activities that will be completed during the session.

Here's a brief overview of the process:

- *Session 1: Introduction to peace and justice ministry.* Introductions, some faith sharing together, scheduling the next gatherings.

- *Session 2: What is Catholic social teaching?* Learning a bit about the Catholic teachings that inspire all peace and justice ministry.

- *Session 3: What types of things might a peace and justice coordinating committee do?* The Catholic bishops of the United States have suggested a framework of different types of peace and justice activities a parish might be involved in. You'll learn those areas of activity, and take an inventory of what's already happening in these areas within your parish.

- *Session 4: What should we call ourselves, and what's our mission?* Coming up with a name and mission statement together will help to focus your ministry.

- *Session 5: What elements should be part of any experience we plan?* Learning about a process called "Discern, Act, Reflect, Transform," which will provide the essential building blocks for any peace and justice activity.

- *Session 6: What's next?* Starting to build an action plan.

Because of the diverse range of parish cultures and setups, details provided for how to conduct the sessions are relatively minimal. But you should have enough information here to lead each session.

For each session, provide a comfortable meeting space, if possible, and consider serving refreshments. (Group members can take turns providing refreshments.)

Facilitators should prepare a five-minute opening prayer for each session. These prayers should connect to events that are happening in the community or world. For instance, in the case of a significant natural disaster overseas, Catholic Relief Services always provides a prayer for those affected. The internet can be a good resource for finding prayers connected to current events. You may want to connect to the liturgical year; there might be a key celebration or saint's feast day near a meeting date that you can use. Key ingredients for prayer together include Scripture, music (preferably sung), words of prayer, and ritual involvement by the participants. This ritual involvement could include faith sharing on Scripture, writing down a place where they encountered God in the past week, or even blessing one another's hands with holy water, connecting the work of peace and justice to baptism.

Facilitators should also prepare a brief closing prayer, which can include the spoken prayer intentions of the committee and an "Our Father" or other prayer.

If possible, at your first gathering, schedule the remaining five sessions about two to three weeks apart.

This process is based on small-group conversation and involvement. Get people chatting with each other, and encourage all to participate in the conversation. If one or more persons dominate the conversation, consider pulling them aside after a meeting and inviting them to try to make sure others have a chance to share.

Consider using name tags at your first several gatherings to encourage participants to use each other's names.

Session 1: Introduction to Peace and Justice Ministry
(60–75 minutes)

Facilitator Notes

Have Bible open to Luke 10:29-37 (the parable of the Good Samaritan).

Materials: Session 1 Handout, one per participant. Download the handout at www.litpress.org/peace-and-justice.

Outline of Session

Personal introductions (15 minutes)
Opening prayer (5 minutes)
Read and discuss "Starting a Peace and Justice Coordinating Committee" (10 minutes)
Read aloud gospel passage and quietly read essay (10 minutes)
Discuss passage and essay (15 minutes)
Announcements/schedule next meetings (5 minutes)
Closing prayer (5 minutes)

Personal Introductions

If the group is new or has added new members, have each participant share his or her name, a little biographical information, and answer *one* of the following get-to-know-you questions:

- If money was no object, what would you do all day?
- What is your favorite book, movie, or song, and why?
- What is one thing you think should be taught in school that's not usually taught in school? Why?
- What is the best gift you've ever been given? Why?
- If you were a superhero, what powers would you have?
- If you could live in any other period in history, which period would you choose? Why?
- What's the most daring thing you have ever done?
- What is your favorite family tradition?

- If you were the ruler of your own country, what is the first law you would introduce?
- What sort of celebration would there be on a "St. *You* Day"?

Opening Prayer

The meeting facilitator leads an opening prayer.

Starting a Peace and Justice Coordinating Committee (read silently)

Thank you for your interest in helping your parish start or rejuvenate a peace and justice coordinating committee! This series of six sessions outlined in this chapter of *The Ministry of Peace and Justice* is meant to help your small group prepare for and undertake this important work. Here is a brief overview of the process:

- *Session 1: Introduction to peace and justice ministry* (you're in it now). Introductions, some faith sharing together, scheduling the next gatherings.
- *Session 2: What is Catholic social teaching?* Learning a bit about the Catholic teachings that inspire all peace and justice ministry.
- *Session 3: What types of things might a peace and justice coordinating committee do?* The Catholic bishops of the United States have suggested a framework of different types of peace and justice activities a parish might be involved in. You'll learn those areas of activity, and take an inventory of what's already happening in these areas within your parish.
- *Session 4: What should we call ourselves, and what's our mission?* Coming up with a name and mission statement together will help to focus your ministry.
- *Session 5: What elements should be part of any experience we plan?* Learning about a process called "Discern, Act,

Reflect, Transform," which will provide the essential building blocks for any peace and justice activity.

- *Session 6: What's next?* Starting to build an action plan.

These sessions should get you talking, reflecting, thinking, and, by the end, planning. Your group might find that particular sessions as they're written here might actually take several different gatherings to work through; don't feel beholden to the suggested structure. For some parishes, it might make sense to spend six months or even a whole year learning, growing as a team, and building a plan before actually coordinating any activities. But the various elements included in these sessions—from learning about Catholic social teaching to crafting a mission statement—should point you in the right direction.

The Catholic bishops of the United States stand with you as you embark on this journey together. In their 1994 document Communities of Salt and Light, they affirm the necessity of active parish-based peace and justice ministries. "In these challenging days, we believe that the Catholic community needs to be more than ever a source of clear moral vision and effective action," they write.

"At a time of rampant individualism, we stand for family and community. At a time of intense consumerism, we insist it is not what we have, but how we treat one another that counts. In an age that does not value permanence or hard work in relationships, we believe marriage is forever and children are a blessing, not a burden. At a time of growing isolation, we remind our nation of its responsibility to the broader world, to pursue peace, to welcome immigrants, to protect the lives of hurting children and refugees. At a time when the rich are getting richer and the poor are getting poorer, we insist the moral test of our society is how we treat and care for the weakest among us," they continue.

"We are called to be the 'salt of the earth' and 'light of the world' in the words of the Scriptures (cf. Mt 5:13-16). This task belongs to every believer and every parish. It cannot be assigned to a few or simply delegated to diocesan or national structures.

The pursuit of justice and peace is an essential part of what makes a parish Catholic" (Introduction).

The church needs you, and she is grateful for your openness to this ministry!

Discuss What You Just Read

Gospel Passage (read aloud)

A reading from the gospel according to St. Luke (10:29-37).

Essay (read silently after proclamation of gospel)

On Session 1 handout.

Questions for Discussion

What struck you most in the essay? Why?

The ministry of peace and justice is all about providing opportunities for parishioners to act compassionately. Have you ever encountered "com-passion" in your life as Henri Nouwen and his coauthors define it?

The Samaritan traveler was on a journey, but noticing the wounded man made him change his plans. What moments or people in your own life have led you here to this meeting?

Announcements/Schedule Next Meetings

Try to schedule the next five meetings every one to two weeks if possible.

Closing Prayer

Facilitator leads a closing prayer.

Session 2: What Is Catholic Social Teaching?
(60–75 minutes)

Facilitator Notes

Before the Session:

A day or two before the session, prepare "Catholic Social Teaching Quotes" sheets. For each theme of Catholic social teaching, select two quotes: one from Scripture and one from the writings of bishops or a pope. Take each quote and print it in large font on an 8.5 x 11 piece of paper (one quote per page). I've selected fourteen quotes that work well, available online at www.litpress .org/peace-and-justice, that you can copy and paste.

Be sure to include the name of the respective theme at the top of each quote sheet.

A few minutes before the session starts, hang each of the quote sheets at eye level around the room where you will gather, using masking tape.

An additional handout for this session may be distributed, one per participant. Download Session 2 Handout at www.litpress .org/peace-and-justice.

Outline of Session

Icebreaker (10 minutes)
Opening prayer (5 minutes)
Read and discuss "What is Catholic Social Teaching?" (10 minutes)
Catholic social teaching stations: Part I (15 minutes); Part II
(25 minutes)
Announcements (5 minutes)
Closing prayer (5 minutes)

Icebreaker

As a group, play the game "Two Truths and a Lie," a fun get-to-know-you exercise.

In this activity, each group member thinks of two interesting true facts about him- or herself (e.g., "I have traveled to X countries," "I once took an interpretive dance class," "I once had a dog named Bear and a cat named Rhino").

Each group member also thinks up one "false fact" about him- or herself—something that sounds plausible, but isn't actually true.

Everyone writes down all three of their own "facts" in any order, and then takes turns sharing them aloud.

For each participant, the other group members see if they can guess which "fact" is really the lie. After a short discussion, the group informally votes for one of the three "facts," and then the person whose turn it is reveals which of the "facts" is actually untrue.

Opening Prayer

The meeting facilitator leads an opening prayer.

What Is Catholic Social Teaching? (read silently)

On Session 2 handout.

Discuss What You Just Read

Catholic Social Teaching Stations

Part I:

Fourteen CST quotes sheets are hanging around the room, two per theme.

Circulate around the room on your own, reading the different quotes.

Pick one quote that stands out to you. Reflect quietly on these questions:

- Why does this quote stand out to you?
- What current global event or trend might this quote speak to?
- Think of one way this quote could have an impact on your daily life.

Share these reflections in small groups of two to three when everyone has finished.

Part II:

Assign individuals or small groups to each theme so that all seven themes are covered. (Nobody should have more than one theme assignment.)

As a group (or as an individual, depending on the size of your committee), revisit the two quote stations for your particular theme.

Read the section of chapter 2 of *The Ministry of Peace and Justice* that addresses your theme.

Together as a small group, respond to these prompts:

- Write a definition of your assigned theme. Do not use more than two sentences.

- Come up with one to two current events (or events in recent history) that are somehow related to your theme.

- Think of at least one way you might act on your theme in your own daily life. Think of at least one way your parish might act on your theme.

- Write one to two questions that, if you spent some time exploring, could help you go deeper into your theme. (Don't try to answer these questions now.)

Each small group briefly shares their reflections with the whole group.

Announcements

Confirm next meeting time.

For further reading on CST, find the "Compendium of the Social Doctrine of the Church" printed on the Vatican's website, which addresses these seven themes and others in much more detail. (A quick Google search will bring you there.)

Also, Catholic Relief Services has a series of YouTube videos called CST 101. With one short video per theme, these can be helpful tools for refreshing your memory about all seven.[1]

See if you can memorize the titles of the seven themes by the next time you gather!

Closing Prayer

Facilitator leads a closing prayer.

Session 3: What Types of Things Might a Peace and Justice Coordinating Committee Do? (60–75 minutes)

Facilitator Notes

Materials needed for this session are: six sheets of large easel/ butcher paper; marker; and copies of the Session 3 Handout, one per participant. Download the handout at www.litpress .org/peace-and-justice.

Outline of Session

Opening prayer (5 minutes)
Recap of Catholic social teaching themes (15 minutes)
Read and discuss "What Types of Things Might a Peace and
    Justice Coordinating Committee Do?" (15 minutes)
Peace and justice inventory (20 minutes)
Announcements (5 minutes)
Closing prayer (5 minutes)

Opening Prayer

The meeting facilitator leads an opening prayer.

Recap of Catholic Social Teaching Themes

Review the seven themes of Catholic social teaching. As a refresher, have participants share the definitions of the themes they came up with at the last session.

If video capability is possible, consider viewing the YouTube video "Catholic Social Teaching in 3 Minutes."

What Types of Things Might a Peace and Justice Coordinating Committee Do? (read silently)

On Session 3 handout.

Discuss What You Just Read

Peace and Justice Inventory

On each of six large sheets of butcher paper, write one of the six areas of peace and justice ministry across the top. Hang these up on the wall with masking tape, if possible.

One by one, go through the six areas and take an inventory of what your parish already does. List activities, initiatives, ministry groups, etc., on a bulleted list on each page. Some areas might have numerous entries, while others might have few, if any.

Take a look at the six sheets, and as a group, use any or all of these discussion questions:

- What is the parish doing a lot of already? Are many different people involved in these ministries you've listed, or is it the same few volunteers doing each?

- What area/s of the six does/do not have as many examples?

- Why do you think some of the areas have more examples and some have fewer?

- Who are some of the key people in these existing ministries? Could we invite them to join this committee?

- Which of the areas do you think would be a challenge for your parish to participate in? Why?

- Which area is of most interest to you as an individual member of this committee? Which one are you drawn to?

Be sure to transcribe the inventoried ministries onto notebook paper or on a computer so you might have a record of them.

Announcements

Confirm the group's next meeting time.

Consider inviting a new person or two to join you at your next meeting if there seem to be some key stakeholders in any of the ministries that are already going at your parish.

Closing Prayer

Facilitator leads a closing prayer.

Session 4: What Should We Call Ourselves, and What's Our Mission? (60–75 minutes)

Facilitator Notes

If possible, have a large piece of paper (or whiteboard) and marker available for the session.

You will also want enough copies of both handouts for this session for each participant. Download both at www.litpress.org /peace-and-justice.

Outline of Session

Opening prayer (5 minutes)
Recap: Six areas of peace and justice ministry (5 minutes)
Read and discuss "What Should We Call Ourselves?" (20 minutes)
Read and discuss "What's Our Mission?" (35 minutes)
Announcements (5 minutes)
Closing prayer (5 minutes)

Opening Prayer

The meeting facilitator leads an opening prayer.

Recap: Six Areas of Peace and Justice Ministry

Look at the six areas of social ministry covered in the previous session. One by one, describe what each area entails, and call to mind some of the examples of activities that are already happening in your parish.

What Should We Call Ourselves? (read silently)

On Session 4, handout 1.

Discuss What You Just Read

As a group, make a list of potential names for your group.

Get any and all ideas out there, and record them on large paper or some sort of board for all to see, if possible.

Discuss the ideas. It might be helpful to get easy parts out of the way first. Do you want to use the word "coordinating" or not? Do you want to call yourselves a committee, or something else? Then, you can spend the bulk of your time on the descriptive portion of your committee's name.

Once you come up with a name your group feels good about, move on to the next section.

What's Our Mission? (read silently)

On Session 4, handout 2.

After Reading

Invite one volunteer to serve as a scribe for this portion of the meeting, recording the various ideas that come up.

As you did in the naming process, identify some key terms and phrases that come to mind. List these and do not evaluate them at first. Some examples: "prayer, education, action"; "co-ordinates activities"; "encourages parishioners"; etc.

Discuss the ideas that emerge and try to take these phrases and use them to craft a series of one-sentence mission statement options. Come up with as many as the group needs, even five to ten.

If time allows, narrow down the options and discuss and tweak the remaining possibilities.

If time runs short, invite group members to take the list of options home and think on it. Try to finalize it together at your next meeting.

Announcements

Confirm next meeting time.

Closing Prayer

Facilitator leads a closing prayer.

Session 5: What Elements Should Be Part of Anything We Plan? (60–75 minutes)

Facilitator Notes

Bring a copy of the mission statement to the meeting with you, write it on a poster or whiteboard, and display it for the duration of the meeting.

An additional handout for this session may be distributed, one per participant. Download Session 5 Handout at www.litpress .org/peace-and-justice.

Session Outline

Opening prayer (5 minutes)
Recap mission statement (10 minutes)
Read and discuss "The DART Method of Social Ministry"
    (25 minutes)
Test-drive the DART method (25 minutes)
Announcements (5 minutes)
Closing prayer (5 minutes)

Opening Prayer

The meeting facilitator leads an opening prayer.

Recap Mission Statement

If you completed your mission statement during the last meeting, take a look at it and see if anyone would like to offer any tweaks. If not, practice reciting it in pairs.

If you did not complete your mission statement last time, spend the first part of this session finalizing it.

The DART Method of Social Ministry (read silently)

On Session 5 handout.

Discuss What You Just Read

Are the four steps of the DART Method clear? Any parts that are confusing or could use more explanation?

Test-Drive the DART Method

Either as a whole group or in small groups of three to four, practice using the DART Method.

- *Discern:* What social issues are pressing in your community or nearby? What organizations have you heard of that are working on those issues?

- *Act:* What sort of action step might your committee organize to address this particular issue? Who from the parish would be invited to participate?

- *Reflect:* Come up with at least one sensory, social, and theological reflection question you would want to ask participants after the action experience.

- *Transform:* Think of at least one personal, interpersonal, and structural transformation element that could be a follow-up after the action and reflection steps.

If you broke up into small groups, each group should share their DART process with the whole committee.

Announcements

Confirm the next meeting time.

Closing Prayer

Facilitator leads a closing prayer.

Session 6: What's Next? (60–75 minutes)

Facilitator Notes

If possible, large easel-style paper and a marker should be provided.

An additional handout for this session may be distributed, one per participant. Download Session 6 Handout at www.litpress .org/peace-and-justice.

Outline of Session

Opening prayer (5 minutes)
Recap the DART method (10 minutes)
"What's Next?" activity (50 minutes): Read "What's Next?" (5 minutes); Areas of peace and justice ministry: Brainstorm (25 minutes); Building a preliminary calendar (20 minutes)
Announcements (5 minutes)
Closing prayer (5 minutes)

Opening Prayer

The meeting facilitator leads an opening prayer.

Recap the DART Method

Move step-by-step through the DART Method, covered during the last session. Take a few minutes to describe each step, making sure all participants remember and understand the elements of the process.

What's Next? (read silently)

Areas of Peace and Justice Ministry: Brainstorm

Invite someone to volunteer to serve as a timer, and someone to serve as a recorder.

For each of the six areas of peace and justice ministry, give the group four minutes—no more and no less.

During each four-minute period, participants voice potential activities that fall within the area of social ministry you're working on. These ideas should emerge from any "Discern" work you've done over the last two sessions, and should help the group further its mission statement.

This is not a time to discuss the merits of any particular idea; the recorder should just list them, preferably on large paper for all to see.

Building a Preliminary Calendar

Look over the "Important Peace and Justice Days and Seasons" list (on handout) so it's in the back of your mind.

Discuss the ideas that surfaced during the brainstorm process, and see which three to six ideas rise to the surface. (This narrowing down process could possibly require another meeting at a later date.)

If possible, reproduce the calendar grid found on the next page on a large piece of easel paper or whiteboard.

Plug the group's preferred activities into the grid, placing each in its appropriate month and area of social ministry. (Allow at least two to three months of additional planning time before the first activity.)

Evaluate the selected activities based on time of year and area of social ministry. Are they at good times of the year for the parish? Are at least two to three different areas of social ministry covered?

Announcements

Confirm the group's next meeting time, during which you will start to plan the details of the first activity on your calendar.

Before the next session, read chapter 5 of *The Ministry of Peace and Justice*, which includes some detailed tips for how to plan an individual activity.

Closing Prayer

Facilitator leads a closing prayer.

	Prayer	Education	Outreach	Advocacy	Organizing	Solidarity
January						
February						
March						
April						
May						
June						
July						
August						
September						
October						
November						
December						

Notes

Chapter One

1. Henri Nouwen, Donald P. McNeill, and Douglas A. Morrison, *Compassion: A Reflection on the Christian Life*, rev. ed. (Garden City, NY: Doubleday, 2006), 4.

2. Cornelius Plantinga Jr., "Educating for Shalom: Our Calling as a Christian College," Calvin College, http://www.calvin.edu/about/who-we-are/our-calling.html.

3. Gregory Boyle, *Tattoos on the Heart: The Power of Boundless Compassion* (New York: Free Press, 2010), 188.

4. Address of His Holiness Pope Francis to the Members of the Diplomatic Corps Accredited to the Holy See, January 13, 2014, http://w2.vatican.va/content/francesco/en/speeches/2014/january/documents/papa-francesco_20140113_corpo-diplomatico.html.

5. New York City Rescue Mission, "Have the Homeless Become Invisible?," April 22, 2014, https://www.youtube.com/watch?v=u6jSKLtmYdM.

Chapter Two

1. Jody Rosen, "The Knowledge, London's Legendary Taxi-Driver Test, Puts Up a Fight in the Age of GPS," *New York Times T Magazine*, November 10, 2014, http://tmagazine.blogs.nytimes.com/2014/11/10/london-taxi-test-knowledge/?_r=0.

2. "5 Weeks Pregnant," What to Expect, http://www.whattoexpect.com/pregnancy/week-by-week/week-5.aspx.

3. Alexander Tsiaras, "Conception to Birth—Visualized," TED Talk, December 2010, http://www.ted.com/talks/alexander_tsiaras_conception_to_birth_visualized.

4. Annie Murphy Paul, "What We Learn Before We're Born," TED Talk, July 2011, http://www.ted.com/talks/annie_murphy_paul_what_we_learn_before_we_re_born/.

5. United States Conference of Catholic Bishops (USCCB), The Challenge of Peace: God's Promise and Our Response (May 3, 1983) 15.

6. Randy O'Bannon, "56,662,169 Abortions in America Since Roe vs. Wade in 1973," LifeNews.com, January 12, 2014, http://www.lifenews.com/2014/01/12/56662169-abortions-in-america-since-roe-vs-wade-in-1973/.

7. Michel Martin, "Keeping the Faith in the Catholic Church," Tell Me More, February 15, 2013, http://www.npr.org/2013/02/15/172102690/keeping-the-faith-in-the-catholic-church.

8. Sarah Kaplan, "Has the World 'Looked the Other Way' while Christians Are Killed?," *The Washington Post*, April 7, 2015, http://www.washingtonpost.com/news/morning-mix/wp/2015/04/07/has-the-world-looked-the-other-way-while-christians-are-killed/.

9. "Hunger Statistics," World Food Programme, http://www.wfp.org/hunger/stats.

10. Gwen Dewar, "The Social World of Newborns," http://www.parentingscience.com/newborns-and-the-social-world.html.

11. Homily of John Paul II, November 30, 1986, http://w2.vatican.va/content/john-paul-ii/en/homilies/1986/documents/hf_jp-ii_hom_19861130_perth-australia.html.

12. USCCB, Economic Justice for All: Pastoral Letter on Catholic Social Teaching and the U.S. Economy (1986) 14.

13. USCCB, Forming Consciences for Faithful Citizenship (2007) 13, http://www.usccb.org/issues-and-action/faithful-citizenship/index.cfm.

14. Pope Paul VI, *Populorum Progressio* (March 26, 1967) 65.

15. Carlos Dada, "The Beatification of Óscar Romero," *The New Yorker*, May 19, 2015, http://www.newyorker.com/news/news-desk/the-beatification-of-oscar-romero.

16. Krish Kandiah, "Oscar Romero 35 Years On: Five Quotes You Need to Read from a Modern Day Christian Martyr," *Christian Today*, May 24, 2015, http://www.christiantoday.com/article/oscar.romero.35.years.on.five.quotes.you.need.to.hear.from.a.modern.day.christian.martyr/50651.htm.

17. "Archbishop Oscar Romero: A Bishop for the New Millennium," Introduction, Kellogg Institute at the University of Notre Dame, http://kellogg.nd.edu/romero/Introduction.htm.

18. James Allaire and Rosemary Broughton, "An Introduction to the Life and Spirituality of Dorothy Day," The Catholic Worker Movement, http://www.catholicworker.org/dorothyday/life-and-spirituality.html.

19. Dorothy Day, "Love Is the Measure," *The Catholic Worker*, June 1946, http://www.catholicworker.org/dorothyday/articles/425.html.

20. The Catholic Worker Movement, http://www.catholicworker.org.

21. "Movement to Canonize Dorothy Day," The Dorothy Day Guild, http://dorothydayguild.org/the-cause/movement-to-canonize-dorothy-day/.

22. Kira Dault, "What Is the Preferential Option for the Poor?," *US Catholic*, January 2015, http://www.uscatholic.org/articles/201501/what-preferential-option-poor-29649.

23. Pope Francis, *Evangelii Gaudium*, The Joy of the Gospel (November 24, 2014) 186.

24. USCCB, Federal Budget, http://www.usccb.org/issues-and-action/human-life-and-dignity/federal-budget/.

25. USCCB, Environment/Environmental Justice Program, http://www.usccb.org/issues-and-action/human-life-and-dignity/environment/index.cfm.

26. Pope Paul VI, *Octogesima Adveniens* (May 14, 1971) 23.

27. "Tim's Place, Restaurant Run By 26-Year-Old With Down Syndrome, Serves Hugs With Lunch," *Huffington Post*, June 22, 2012, http://www.huffingtonpost.com/2012/06/22/tim-harris_n_1617057.html.

28. USCCB, The Dignity of Work and Rights of Workers, http://www.usccb.org/beliefs-and-teachings/what-we-believe/catholic-social-teaching/the-dignity-of-work-and-the-rights-of-workers.cfm.

29. Elizabeth O'Hara, "U.S.-Mexico Border Mass Marked by Painful Reunion through the Fence," *Catholic News Service*, November 24, 2014, http://www.catholicnews.com/services/englishnews/2014/u-s-mexico-border-mass-marked-by-painful-reunion-through-the-fence.cfm.

30. John Paul II, *Sollicitudo Rei Socialis* (December 30, 1987) 38.

31. Oscar Cantú and Carolyn Woo, "Letter to Congressional Leaders Regarding Funding for International Poverty-Reducing Humanitarian and Development Assistance," March 9, 2015, http://www.usccb.org/issues-and-action/human-life-and-dignity/global-issues/letter-to-congressional-leaders-from-bishop-cantu-and-crs-on-foreign-appropriations-2015-03-09-11.cfm.

32. Suzanne Goldenberg, "Climate Change: The Poor Will Suffer Most," *The Guardian*, March 30, 2014, http://www.theguardian.com/environment/2014/mar/31/climate-change-poor-suffer-most-un-report.

33. USCCB, Global Climate Change: A Plea for Dialogue, Prudence, and the Common Good, June 15, 2001, http://www.usccb.org/issues-and-action/human-life-and-dignity/environment/global-climate-change-a-plea-for-dialogue-prudence-and-the-common-good.cfm.

Chapter Three

1. Communities of Salt and Light includes a seventh area of peace and justice ministry, "Supporting the 'Salt of the Earth': Family, Work, Citizenship." There are some good insights included in this section of the document about encouraging parishioners to live justly in their everyday lives, but it doesn't fit in neatly here as a distinct area of social ministry.

2. Communities of Salt and Light uses the term "social ministry" instead of "peace and justice ministry"; these can be used interchangeably for our purposes.

3. USCCB, Communities of Salt and Light: Reflections on the Social Mission of the Parish, 1994, http://www.usccb.org/beliefs-and-teachings /what-we-believe/catholic-social-teaching/communities-of-salt-and-light -reflections-on-the-social-mission-of-the-parish.cfm.

4. Benedict XVI, *Deus Caritas Est* (December 25, 2005) 14.

5. USCCB, Sacraments and Social Mission, http://www.usccb.org/prayer -and-worship/sacraments-and-sacramentals/sacraments-and-social-mission .cfm.

6. Kristi Haas, "Grace Before Meals." Used with permission of the author.

7. USCCB, The Challenge of Forming Consciences for Faithful Citizen-ship, 2007, http://www.usccb.org/issues-and-action/faithful-citizenship /upload/Forming-Consciences-Faithful-Citizenship-bulletin-insert.pdf.

8. Ibid.

9. Keith B. Richburg, "N.J. Approves Abolition of Death Penalty; Corzine to Sign," *The Washington Post*, December 14, 2007, http://www .washingtonpost.com/wp-dyn/content/article/2007/12/13/AR2007 121301302.html.

10. Catholic Campaign for Human Development, "Who We Are," http://www.usccb.org/about/catholic-campaign-for-human-development /who-we-are.cfm.

11. Information submitted to me by Ann Heekin through an online "Ministry of Peace and Justice" survey form, March 18, 2015. Used with permission.

12. Cheryl Mrazik and Katie Kernich, "Five Tips for Building Global Solidarity at Your Parish," *The Ampersand*, June 16, 2014, https://camden lifejustice.wordpress.com/2014/06/16/five-tips-for-building-global -solidarity-at-your-parish/. Used with permission.

Chapter Four

1. "A Thing Worth Doing," American Chesterton Society, http:// www.chesterton.org/a-thing-worth-doing/.

2. Edward DeBerri and James Hug, *Catholic Social Teaching: Our Best Kept Secret* (Maryknoll, NY: Orbis, 2003).

3. World Health Organization, "Sierra Leone," http://www.who.int /countries/sle/en/.

4. The Catholic Diocese of Richmond, "The DART Method of Social Ministry," http://www2.richmonddiocese.org/osm/our-social-mission /documents/DART-Summary-2011.pdf.

5. T. S. Eliot, "The Dry Salvages," in *Four Quartets* (Orlando, FL: Houghton Mifflin Harcourt, 2014), 39.

Chapter Five

1. Jeffry Odell Korgen, *My Lord & My God: Engaging Catholics in Social Ministry* (Mahwah, NJ: Paulist Press, 2007), 17–18.

2. Vivian Giang, "The 'Two Pizza Rule' Is Jeff Bezos' Secret to Productive Meetings," *Business Insider*, October 29, 2013, http://www.business insider.com/jeff-bezos-two-pizza-rule-for-productive-meetings-2013-10.

3. Pat Slater, "Seven Tips for Parish Social Ministry," *The Ampersand*, July 16, 2014, https://camdenlifejustice.wordpress.com/2014/07/16 /seven-tips-for-parish-social-ministry/.

4. Information from Laura Flanagan submitted to me through an online "Ministry of Peace and Justice" survey form, March 3, 2015. Used with permission.

5. USCCB, Unity in Diversity: A Scriptural Rosary, http://www.justice forimmigrants.org/documents/Scriptural-Rosary-Eng.pdf.

6. *Faith in Action*, Paulist Evangelization Ministries, http://www.pemdc .org/Faith-in-Action-Participant-Booklet.aspx.

7. Jack Jezreel, "Best Practices for Charity and Justice," *U.S. Catholic* (March 2014): 30–31.

Chapter Six

1. "CST 101: Catholic Social Teaching," YouTube playlist, by Catholic Relief Services, https://www.youtube.com/playlist?list=PLt5PsPjJAk -0b9BYRHUAxnlKMIv7qyZca.